Lipreading

Edward F. Walther

NELSON-HALL nh CHICAGO

LIBRARY OF CONGRESS CATALOGING IN PUBLICATION DATA

Walther, Edward F.
  Lipreading.

  1. Lipreading.   I. Title.
HV2487.W33   371.91'27   81-14196
ISBN 0-88229-523-3   AACR2

Manufactured in the United States of America

10 9 8 7 6 5 4 3 2 1

The paper in this book is pH neutral (acid-free).

Contents

Preface

This book is written from my own observations and experiences as a person who became hard of hearing in later years and taught lipreading for over ten years as a lay teacher at the Chicago Hearing Society. I hope to be able to help the many elderly as well as young deaf persons who live in areas that do not have the necessary facilities to teach lipreading. I also hope to provide material and guidance to help teachers of the hard of hearing.

A blind person with a red and white cane or a crippled person with crutches outwardly displays to other people that he or she may sometimes require their assistance, and such aid is usually given readily by persons nearby. However, a person who is hard of hearing displays little outward evidence (unless he is wearing a hearing aid, which is hardly noticeable). For this reason he must let others know that he needs help to understand what is being spoken.

Lipreading is an aid to communication that has been used successfully for over three hundred years; its use is mentioned in books written as early as the sixteenth century. Many persons in the past who succeeded and gained fame were deaf.

In my association with the Chicago Hearing Society I have met many persons who are successful in the business world although they are hard of hearing or deaf. Obviously, the reason for their success must be that they are excellent lipreaders and can readily participate in the necessary communication between persons in their positions. Many are able to compete in the business world and have well-adjusted lives even though they are hard of hearing.

I have noticed that when a deaf person is with someone else, the person who is not deaf uses every possible means to make the deaf person understand what he is trying to tell him. If he has a pencil and paper, he writes down his words; if not, he points his finger and writes the words in the air. He may lean over and talk loudly into the deaf person's ear in hopes that he can be understood, or perhaps he goes through the motions of what he is trying to convey. If the deaf person has only a limited ability to lipread and manages to understand the other person, it is possible to have a conversation of which the deaf person comprehends 100 percent.

If another person enters the room and joins the conversation, the deaf person still comprehends a significant part of the conversation for a short period of time. Gradually, however, the conversation is taken over by persons with normal hearing and soon the hard-of-hearing person is left out while the others carry on a conversation he cannot understand.

Imagine three people engaged in a general conversation. Then imagine the predicament one person would be in if a glass enclosure were placed around him so that he could see but not hear what was going on around him.

When a substantial number of people are in a room they tend to cluster in small conversational groups. A hard-of-hearing person, even though he or she might go from group to group, would grasp very little of the conversation and might soon retire to some spot outside the groups and try to find some means of passing the time. At one family gathering of twenty-one persons, I noticed five groups and four different conversations being carried on among them. Any hard-of-hearing person who had no means of understanding others would soon find something else to occupy his mind — perhaps reading a book or looking out the window. If such a person had a limited degree of hearing that could be bolstered with a hearing aid, or could lipread to a fair degree, he could single out one group and direct all his attention to that group. In addition, he must let it be known that he is hard of hearing and needs assistance now and then to keep pace with the general discussion.

It is assumed that a person with a hearing loss is under the care of a competent doctor who specializes in this field. The doctor will decide whether a hearing aid is needed. If the loss is so severe that an aid cannot help enough, the doctor will probably suggest lipreading. In a large city, the deaf person will be directed to an institution with facilities and personnel to teach the art of lipreading. In a smaller town, lipreading instruction is usually not available. This book is written to help teach the art of lipreading to persons who cannot attend lipreading classes.

This is a self-help book, and there are several ways in which it may be used. One method, obviously, is to seat yourself before a mirror and do the exercises. Read the words or sentences silently at moderate speed, and watch and memorize lip movements carefully.

Even more effective is having another person silently read the words or sentences. This is how it is done in lipreading classrooms. Each session should last at least thirty minutes—more if your helper is patient. Two or three exercise sessions a week will bring surprising results.

Of course, don't limit your lipreading to the time you spend with a book. Watch the lips of people who appear on television shows and the lips of those you converse with. Lipreading is a full-time experience; nothing can take the place of practice and more practice.

Acknowledgments

Many thanks to Karen Kirschbaum for her lip formation photographs and to the Chicago Hearing Society, whose tutoring and help have enabled me to help others.

1. Teach Yourself to Lipread

As a person's deafness increases, his contact with other persons may decrease, depending on the amount he can hear and understand. A person who can lipread will find little change in his social life, for his ability to lipread permits him to communicate almost as he did when his hearing was normal.

You can teach yourself to lipread. Practically any person with normal intelligence can do so. You must overcome several obstacles, but as you progress and increase your skill at lipreading, these obstacles will lessen one by one.

The first obstacle to overcome is the loss of one of the five senses. From the time a person is born until his hearing declines, he depends on his sense of hearing. In lipreading this sense is transferred to the sense of seeing; your eyes become your ears. You must constantly watch the face of the person speaking to you. When you are first learning, lipreading requires considerable concentration. As you progress, the effort required decreases, and concentrating on the person speaking to you soon becomes natural and comes more easily.

The second obstacle is the problem of homophonous words. Homophonous words are words that have the same lip movement but are spelled differently and have entirely different meanings. For example, the words *jade* and *shade* have identical lip movement although their spellings and meanings are not the same. Likewise the words *pail* and *mail*. Always try to have a good idea of the topic of conversation, as it helps you figure out what homophonous word is being used. You can also tell what homophonous word is being used from its context in the sentence.

A third obstacle is that some letters of the alphabet are pronounced without any lip movements. All letters that are pronounced as throat sounds are unseen. Sounds that are formed by the tongue are normally unseen, but sometimes if the person speaking uses a well-formed lip movement, they can be seen. Examples are *th, l, d, n, nt, nd,* which involve a tongue movement to the palate or upper teeth. Chapter 87 explains sounds that have no lip movements.

All speech involves the passage of air through the throat and out the mouth. The changes in sound are made as the air passes over or around the tongue and various formations of the lips. For example, to speak the word *call,* the following movements are made for the passage of air:

1. *c* — the back of the tongue closes against the throat just above the esophagus.
2. *a* — the lips open wide with a slight pucker at the corners.
3. *ll* — the tip of the tongue touches behind the upper teeth.

Any person who speaks this word must make the same movements varying only slightly with his personal manner of speaking. If the word is spoken in a loud voice, more movement is used; as the volume decreases, less lip movement is used; but every word spoken requires the same throat, tongue, and lip movements from each person who speaks the word. You will have more contact with some people than others. As a lipreader, you must analyze the form and manner a given person uses to deliver speech. As you progress in lipreading you will find yourself placing these persons in various categories according to what you must look for in their lip movements.

In lipreading, you are concerned with the *pronunciation* of each word rather than with its spelling. If you look in a dictionary, you will find each word spelled out, followed by its pronunciation spelled phonetically. In many cases the pronunciation is "spelled" differently from the word itself. The word *flood*, for example, is pronounced *flŭd*, with a short *u* sound. The word *scion,* which ends in *-cion,* is pronounced *sī ən,* while *coercion,* which also ends in *-cion,* ends with the sound *shun* or *shən.* In the word *through,* the *ou* has the long *oo* sound and the *gh* is not pronounced (*thrōō*). In the word *rough,* on the other hand, the *ou* has the short *u* sound, and the *gh* is pronounced like an *f* (*rŭf*).

One symbol used in phonetic pronunciations is the *schwa* (ə). It indicates an indeterminate vowel sound for unstressed syllables of English. For example, the *e* in *system* (*sĭs'-təm*).

Pronunciation may vary in different parts of the country. People in the South, for example, often say *ah* in words that would be pronounced with a long *i* by persons from the North.

The important point, again, is that the pronunciation, not the spelling, is what you must be aware of as a lipreader. When lipreading use and think of the phonetic pronunciation, as the person speaking to you uses this lip movement.

The lipreader has the following facts in his favor. A normal, intelligent conversation can be carried on with the knowledge and use of only about five to six hundred words. In daily conversation many words are used over and over again. Prepositions and pronouns are the major parts of speech in constant daily use. Furthermore, in normal speech, most speakers use the simplest form of an expression. Most people would say "equal to" rather than "commensurate with," for example.

Also in favor of the lipreader is the fact that a small number of prefixes and suffixes are used with a great number of words to change their tense and meaning. For example, note the changes in the word *test*:

test	Test the electric circuit.
tests	He tests motors at the factory.
tested	He tested ten motors today.
testing	He is testing your motor now.
tester	He is a circuit tester at the factory.
untested	We do not ship an untested motor.

Your time spent on learning the lip movements for these affixes will be well rewarded. As you become more proficient in lipreading the lip movement for affixes becomes almost automatically understood regardless of which basic word is used.

Another advantage for the lipreader is the great number of compound words. In the sections called "Three-Word Drill" are listed numerous compound words. Compound words are made up of other words. In the case of lipreading, compound words are made up of the sounds of other words. The sounds of *fire* and *wood,* for example, make up the word *firewood.* If you learn to lipread *fire* and *wood* you have also learned to lipread *firewood.* Even if the words have entirely unrelated definitions, you should have no problem.

Learning to lipread will require much study on your part. You must make it a daily, constant routine to learn new words and lip formations. Progress at first will be slow, but a definite degree of ability should be noticeable after six months. Your progress depends on your efforts, time, and aptitude. The more effort and study you invest, the greater the results you can expect.

Before you start to learn lipreading, read this book from cover to cover as you would a novel or story. Try to correlate in your mind how one phase of lipreading relates to another phase; then start to learn. As you progress, however, be sure you fully understand each principle or section before proceeding to the next.

2. Lip Movements

Here are some photographs of lip movements that form the basis of lipreading. After you read each description, watch your own lips in a mirror as you say the sounds, or watch another person as he or she pronounces the sounds for you.

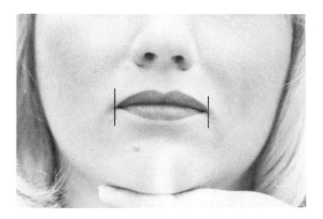

Fig. 1. Lips natural.

The expression "lips natural" means that the position of the lips is that of a person not speaking. Note the vertical lines drawn at the edges of the lips. In the following figures these lines are used to show the lip movement for each vowel or consonant relative to the lips' natural position. The lips' natural position also represents the lip movement for *m, p,* and *b* when these consonants appear in the middle of a word, as in *summer, rapid,* and *labor.*

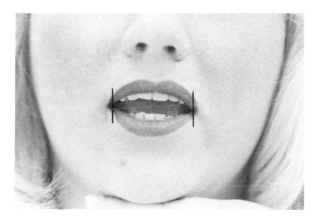

Fig. 2. Short *a*.

For the short *a* (the sound in *hat*) the lips open wide and extend slightly at the corners. This is the widest opening of the extended vowels. Note the vertical lines, which show how the corners extend from the lips' natural position.

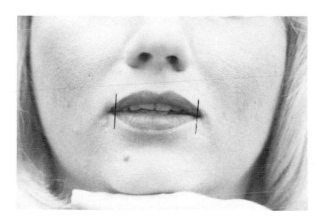

Fig. 3. Short *e*.

For the short *e* (the sound in *met*) the lip opening is medium with a slight extension of the corners of the lips.

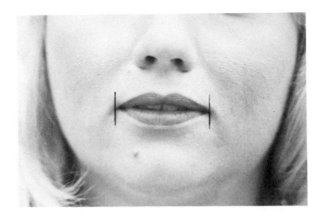

Fig. 4. Short *i*.

For the short *i* (the sound in *hit*) the lip opening is narrow; the corners of the lips remain natural.

Fig. 5. Short *oo*.

For the short *oo* (the sound in *look*) the lip opening is medium; the lips pucker and thrust forward slightly.

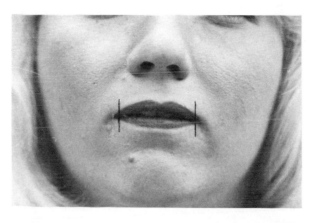

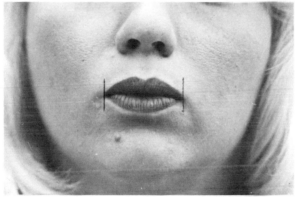

Fig. 6. Diphthong — long *a*.

For the long *a* (the sound in *made*) the lips must make a double movement. First the opening is like that for the short *e,* a medium opening with the corners extended, followed by a quick, natural, narrow opening.

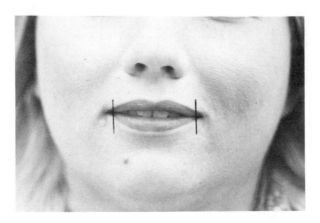

Fig. 7. Long *e*.

For the long *e* (the sound in *me*) the lip opening is narrow and the lips extend at the corners.

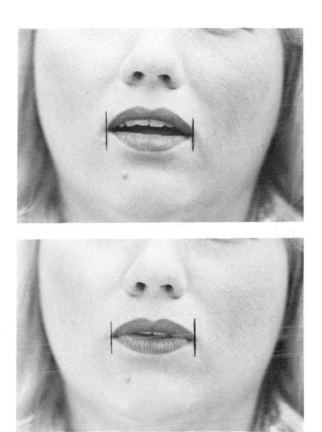

Fig. 8. Diphthong — long *i*.

For the long *i* (the sound in *bite*) the corners of the lips remain natural with a double movement. First is a wide, natural opening, then a quick, natural, narrow movement.

Fig. 9. Relaxed *a*.

For the relaxed or broad *a* or *ah* (the sound in *mart*) the lips remain natural and the opening is the largest of all the relaxed vowels.

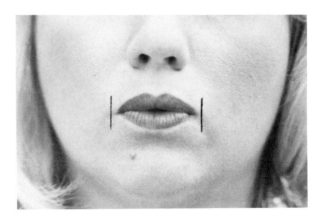

Fig. 10. Long *oo*.

For the long *oo* (the sound in *food*) the lip opening is very narrow and the lips pucker and thrust forward.

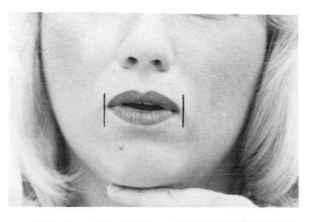

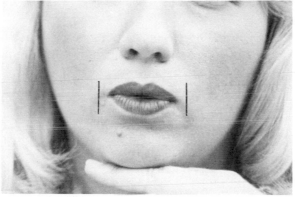

Fig. 11. Diphthong — long *o*.

The long *o* (the sound in *sole*) is a double movement. First the lip opening is wide with a slight puckering, then the lips narrow slightly and become more puckered.

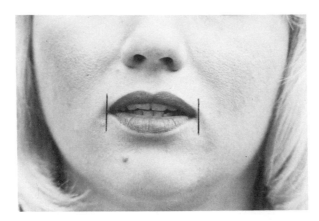

Fig. 12. Short *u* and short *o*.

For the short *u* (the sound in *fun*) the lip opening is medium and the corners of the lip remain natural. For the short *o* (the sound in *hot*) the lip movement is identical to the short *u*.

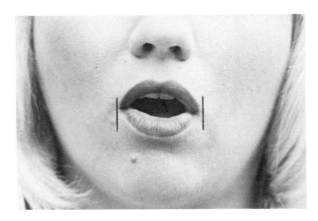

Fig. 13. The *aw* in *raw*, and the *o* in *or*.

For the *aw* (the sound in *raw*) and *o* (the sound in *or*) the lips pucker slightly with a wide opening. The opening is the widest of all the puckered vowels.

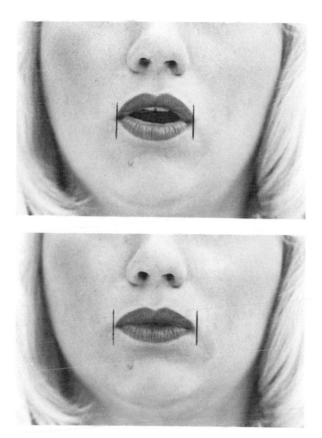

Fig. 14. Diphthong *ow*.

The *ow* (the sound in *plow*) is a double movement; first a relaxed, wide opening, then a very defined puckered movement.

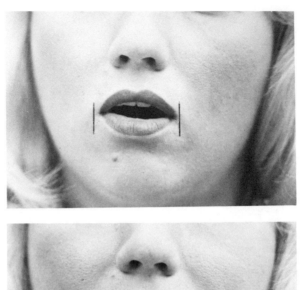
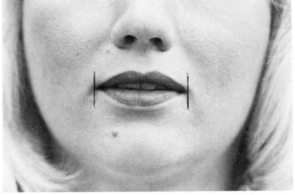

Fig. 15. Diphthong *oy*.

The *oy* (the sound in *toy*) is a double movement. The lips pucker with a wide opening, followed by a quick, natural, narrow movement.

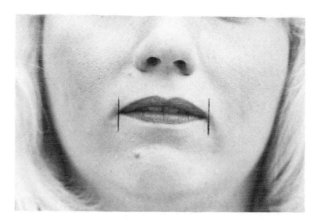

Fig. 16. Consonants *f*, *v*, and *ph*.

For *f*, *v*, and *ph*, the lip opening is narrow and the lower lip touches the upper teeth.

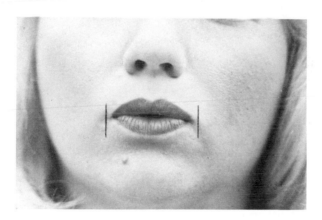

Fig. 17. Consonants *w* and *wh*.

For *w* (as in *wet*) and *wh* (as in *what*), the lips pucker with a very narrow opening.

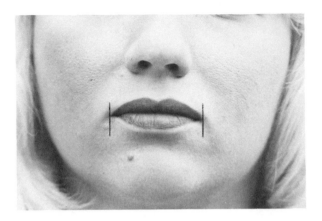

Fig. 18. Consonants *s,* soft *c,* and *z.*

For *s* (as in *sell*), soft *c* (as in *cell*), and *z* (as in *zone*) the lip opening is very narrow, hardly noticeable.

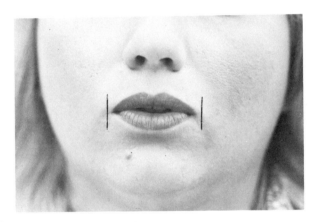

Fig. 19. Consonants *sh, zh, ch, j,* and soft *g.*

For *sh, zh, ch, j,* and soft *g* (as in *gem*) the lip opening is very narrow with lips thrusting forward.

3. Consonant Sounds

Consonant sounds can be grouped according to whether or not they require lip movement.

The following consonants are formed with a lip movement:

b, f, m, p, ph, v, w, wh, r (at the beginning of a word)

The following consonants are formed by breath expiration revealed by a lip movement:

ch, soft *c,* soft *g, j, r, s, sh, z, zh*

The following consonants are formed by the tongue with no lip movement:

d, l, n, t, nd, nt, th

The following consonants are formed with no lip movement:

k, hard *c,* hard *g, ng, nk, y, h*

K and hard *c* are throat sounds; *h* involves an expiration of breath. When *y* is used at the end of a word, its pronunciation changes to short *i.*

4. Learning Your First Words

Seat yourself in front of a mirror, and closely watch the movement of your lips as you speak. As you progress you will also notice a slight movement of the cheeks, the chin, and in some cases the throat (slightly under the chin on both sides of the esophagus). Gently place your thumb and first finger on either side of the esophagus and say the word *coming.* You will notice a slight expansion of the muscle in front of the esophagus when you pronounce the *-ing.*

The first few simple words will be broken down to show the consonants and vowels as they make up a spoken word.

Ready for your first word?

Read the following out loud: *sham.*

Speaking the word *sham* requires three movements:

$$\underline{sh}\ \underline{\breve{a}}\ \underline{m}$$
$$1\quad 2\quad 3$$

1. The *sh* is formed by a very narrow opening with the upper and lower lips thrusting slightly forward.
2. The short *a* is formed with a wide opening of the lips with the corners of the lips slightly drawn back.
3. The *m* is formed by returning the lips to their natural position.

To find the lip movement for any sound, refer to the illustrations in Section 2 and the quick reference guide at the end of the book. Look in the mirror; watch your lip movements closely; speak slowly; and make these three formations with your lips. Notice and feel the lip movements for the *sh*, the short *a*, and the *m*.

Still looking in the mirror, with slightly exaggerated speech movements, slowly speak this word as broken down into three parts. Notice each lip formation in the mirror, and get the feel of it. Repeat the word slowly six or seven times. Now speak the word as you would naturally about ten times, noting the movement as a naturally spoken word.

Can you lipread your first word—*sham*?

The second word is *march*.

$$\underline{m}\ \underline{\ddot{a}r}\ \underline{ch}$$
$$1\quad 23\quad 4$$

Speaking the word requires four movements. Note the italic letters. The *r* is not underscored; it is not seen as a lip movement. In these lessons only the underscored words have lip movements. The numbers underneath will denote the separate movements used to pronounce the word.

1. The *m* is formed by a slight pressure of the closed upper and lower lips.
2. The relaxed *a* is formed by a wide opening of the lips with the lips slightly extended at the corners.
3. The *r* sound in the middle of a word is made by a slight opening of the lips and a roll of the tongue. It is slurred over and often will show no movement.
4. The *ch* is formed by a very narrow opening with the upper and lower lips thrusting slightly forward.

Look in the mirror: watch your lip movements closely; speak slowly, and make these four formations with your lips and tongue. Notice and feel the lip movement for the *m*, the relaxed *a*, the *r*, and the *ch*. Note that the *a* and *r* blend together.

Still looking in the mirror, with slightly exaggerated speech movements, slowly speak this word as broken down into four parts. Notice each lip formation in the mirror and get the feel of it. Repeat slowly six or seven times; then speak the word as you would normally, noting the movements as they would usually appear in speech.

The third word is *fifth*. Speaking it requires four movements:

$$\underline{f} \ \underline{\breve{\imath}} \ \underline{f} \ \underline{th}$$
$$1 \ \ 2 \ \ 3 \ \ 4$$

1. The *f* is formed by a narrow opening of the lips with the upper teeth touching the lower lip.
2. The short *i* is made with a narrow lip opening.
3. (Same as number 1.)
4. The *th* is made with a slight opening of the lips and the tongue touching the upper teeth.

Now look in the mirror; watch your lip movements closely; speak slowly; and make these four formations with your lips. Notice and feel the lip movement for the *f*, the short *i*, and the *th*.

Still looking in the mirror, with slightly exaggerated speech movements, slowly speak the word as broken down into four parts. Notice each formation in the mirror and get the feel of the lip movement. You should note that the *th* is almost invisible, but you can feel your tongue touch your teeth. Repeat slowly six or seven times. Now speak the word as you would naturally about ten times, noting the visible movement and the feel of the tongue touching the teeth for the *th*.

The fourth word is *action*. Speaking it requires four movements. Remember that lipreading is based on the pronunciation of a word rather than its spelling. Action is pronounced *ăk-shən*. This pronunciation determines the lip movements used. (Note that the *io* takes the *uh*.)

$$\underline{\breve{a}k} \ \underline{sh} \ \underline{\partial} \ \underline{n}$$
$$1 \ \ \ 2 \ \ 3 \ \ 4$$

1. The short *a* and the *k* blend, the short *a* movement is quickly followed by the *k,* which is a throat sound not seen on the lips.

2. The *sh* is formed by a very narrow opening with the upper and lower lips thrusting slightly forward.

3. The schwa (ə) is made with a medium opening of the lips.

4. The *n* is unseen, sounded by the tongue touching the palate behind the upper teeth.

Look in the mirror and, watching your lip movement closely, speak slowly and make these four formations with your lip and tongue. Notice the lip movement for the *ăk, sh, ə,* and *n.*

Still looking in the mirror, with slightly exaggerated speech movements, speak this word as broken down into four parts. Notice each lip formation and get the feel of the lip and tongue movement. Repeat seven or eight times. Now speak the word as you would naturally about ten times, noting the movements as they appear in a naturally spoken word.

The fifth word is *import.* A dictionary will show that the word has two syllables, divided like this: *im-port.* The syllable break means that the *m* and *p* are individual sounds. Speaking the word requires four movements:

$$\frac{ĭ \quad m \quad p \quad ō \quad rt}{1 \quad 2 \quad 3 \quad 4 \quad 5}$$

1. The short *i* is made with a narrow opening of the lips.

2. For the *m* the lips return to their natural position with a slight pause for:

3. The *p,* which is again made with the lips natural.

4. For the *o* the lips pucker, with a medium to wide opening, then become more puckered.

5. The *rt* is an unseen blend sounded by a roll of the tongue to the palate.

Looking in the mirror and watching lip movements closely, speak slowly and make the five formations with your lips. Notice the five movements carefully.

Still looking in the mirror, with slightly exaggerated speech movements, slowly speak the word as broken down into five parts. Notice the lip formations, and get the feel of the lip and tongue movements.

Repeat about ten times. Now speak the word as you would naturally, noting the movements as they would appear in normal conversation.

The sixth word is *phantom*. The phonetic pronunciation is *făn-təm*. In lipreading, the word has five movements:

$$\underline{f} \ \underline{\breve{a}} \ nt \ \underline{\text{ə}m}$$
$$1 \ 2 \ 3 \ \ 45$$

1. The *f* is made with a narrow opening of the lips and the upper teeth touching the lower lip.
2. For the *ă*, the lips open wide, with the corners slightly drawn back. The opening is the widest of the extended vowels.
3. The *nt* is curved together, unseen, and the sound is made by the tongue touching the palate.
4. The *əm* has the short *u* sound, a medium opening of the lips. The *m* is formed in the lips natural position.
5. Follow the procedure given for previous words to study the lip movements, and get the feel of the word formation.

Now use the same procedures, including the reference aids in Section 2 and the quick reference guide, to practice lipreading these words:

pamper	$\underline{p} \ \underline{\breve{a}} \ \underline{m} \ \underline{p} \ \underline{\text{ə}r}$
	1 2 3 4 5
show	$\underline{sh} \ \underline{\bar{o}}$
	1 2
beach	$\underline{b} \ \underline{\bar{e}} \ \underline{ch}$
	1 2 3
match	$\underline{m} \ \underline{\breve{a}} \ \underline{ch}$
	1 2 3
thumb	$\underline{th} \ \underline{\breve{u}} \ \underline{m}$
	1 2 3
home	$\underline{h} \ \underline{\bar{o}} \ \underline{m}$
	1 2

Note that when *h* or hard *c* appears at the beginning of a word, its sound is made in the throat with a breath expiration and no movement is seen on the lips. The only evidence is a slight falling of the chest. These consonants require breath expiration and cannot be spoken while inhaling.

$$\text{impeach} \quad \underline{\breve{i}\ m\ p}\ \underline{\bar{e}}\ \underline{ch}$$
$$\qquad\qquad\quad 1\ 2\ 3\ 4\ 5$$

$$\text{jam} \quad \underline{j}\ \underline{\breve{a}}\ \underline{m}$$
$$\qquad\quad 1\ 2\ 3$$

$$\text{jeep} \quad \underline{j}\ \underline{\bar{e}}\ p$$
$$\qquad\quad 1\ 2\ 3$$

$$\text{ketch} \quad k\ \underline{\breve{e}}\ \underline{ch}$$
$$\qquad\qquad 1\ \ 2$$

$$\text{life} \quad l\ \underline{\bar{i}}\ \underline{f}$$
$$\qquad\quad 1\ 2\ 3$$

When *l, t,* or *d* is used at the beginning of a word, the movement is a slight opening of the lips with the tongue touching behind the upper teeth. When the person speaking to you has excellent pronunciation, this movement is sometimes noticeable, giving considerable help in lipreading.

$$\text{mayhem} \quad \underline{m}\ \underline{\bar{a}}\ h\ \underline{\breve{e}}\ \underline{m}$$
$$\qquad\qquad\quad 1\ 2\ \ \ 3\ 4$$

$$\text{phone} \quad \underline{f}\ \underline{\bar{o}}\ n$$
$$\qquad\qquad 1\ 2$$

$$\text{random} \quad \underline{r}\ \underline{\breve{a}}\ n\ \underline{d}\ \partial\ \underline{m}$$
$$\qquad\qquad\quad 1\ 2\ 3\ 4\ \ \ 5$$

For *r* in *random* the lips pucker or draw in at the corners; for the *n* and *d* the tongue touches behind the upper teeth. Only the *a, a,* and *m* are revealed by lip movement.

$$\text{speed} \quad \underline{s}\ \underline{p}\ \underline{\bar{e}}\ d$$
$$\qquad\qquad 1\ 2\ 3\ 4$$

Speed is another word in which not all the letters show lip movement. The *p* and *e* are visible. The *s* sound requires a very narrow, quick opening of the lips, hardly seen in normal speech. In these cases the context of the word in the sentence is of help.

We are in a twenty mile-per-hour speed zone.

$$
\begin{array}{cccc}
\text{vamp} & \dfrac{v}{1} & \dfrac{\breve{a}}{2} & \dfrac{m}{3} & \dfrac{p}{4}
\end{array}
$$

$$
\begin{array}{ccc}
\text{wide} & \dfrac{w}{1} & \dfrac{\bar{i}}{2} & \dfrac{d}{3}
\end{array}
$$

Every word that you speak can be broken down in the foregoing manner to help you recognize the lip movement and get the feel of the word. The expression "the feel of the word" means the feeling in your mouth of the lip movement, the tongue touching the palate or teeth, the roll of the tongue with breath expiration, and the throat sounds.

5. Learning Longer Words

The following words have more than two syllables. They are given as an aid for future reference to help you master longer words:

$$
\begin{array}{cccc}
\text{automobile} & \dfrac{\hat{o}}{1} & \dfrac{t\partial}{2} & \dfrac{m\partial}{3} & \dfrac{b\bar{e}l}{4}
\end{array}
$$

Here are the movements, divided by syllables:
1. The *ô* may sound like *ah* or *aw*, depending on the speaker.
2. The *t* and *ə* slur together. The *t* is made by the tongue touching the palate, flowing into the *ə* vowel sound.
3. The *m* is made in the lips-natural position, again flowing into the *ə* vowel sound.
4. The *h* is formed with lips natural; for the long *e* the lips are extended with a narrow opening; and for the *l*, the tongue is touching the upper teeth.

Pronounce the word slowly, all four syllables, to get the feel of the lip and tongue movements for the entire word. Now, looking in the mirror, speak the word as you would naturally to get the feel of the tongue and see the lip movements in the mirror. Repeat the word, watching your lip movements as many times as necessary, until you recognize the word as naturally spoken.

condensation $\underline{k\breve{o}n}$ $\underline{d\breve{e}n}$ $\underline{s\bar{a}}$ $\underline{sh\partial n}$
$\qquad\qquad\qquad\quad$ 1 $\quad$ 2 $\quad$ 3 $\quad$ 4

Condensation is a four syllable word. Each syllable is broken down to show the movements.

1. The *k* is an unseen throat sound; the *o* has the short *o* sound as in *box*, which is formed by a wide opening of the lips; the *n* is unseen, the tongue touching the palate.
2. The *d* is unseen, with tongue touching the palate; the short *e* is formed by a medium opening of the lips with the corners extending; the *n* is unseen, the tongue touching the palate again.
3. The *s* is almost visible, formed with a very narrow opening of the lips. The long *a* is made with a medium extended opening, followed quickly by a relaxed, narrow movement.
4. The *sh* is made with a thrust forward of the lips, with a narrow, slightly puckered opening. The *ə* is pronounced *uh*, being a natural, medium opening of the lips. The *n* is unseen, tongue touching the palate.

It is not necessary to break a word down in this manner, but it helps illustrate the separate lip and tongue movements of a word.

Pronounce *condensation* slowly, all four syllables, to get the feel of the lip and tongue movements. Looking in the mirror, speak the word as you would naturally, noting what movements are visible. Repeat the word as many times as necessary until you recognize *condensation* as a naturally spoken word. Remember that the italicized vowels and consonants are the only ones seen as lip movements.

legislation $\underline{l\breve{e}j}$ $\underline{\breve{i}s}$ $\underline{l\bar{a}}$ $\underline{sh\partial n}$
$\qquad\qquad\qquad\quad$ 1 $\quad$ 2 $\quad$ 3 $\quad$ 4 5
speaking requires five movements

1. The *l* is formed by the tongue touching the palate; the short *e* is made with the lips open medium wide and slightly extended at the corners; the *j* is made with the lips narrowly open, puckered, and thrust forward.
2. For the short *i*, the lips are narrowly open with the corners re-

maining natural; the *s* is hard to see—it is made with a very narrow opening and a hiss sound.

3. The *l* is made by the tongue touching the palate; for the long *a* the lips open medium wide, then form a natural opening.

4,5. For the *sh* the lips have a narrow opening, puckered and thrust forward; the *ə* takes the short *u* sound, a natural medium opening of the lips; for the *n*, the tongue touches the palate.

Again pronounce the word slowly, noting the seen and unseen lip movements and getting the feel of the unseen movements. Repeat the word as naturally spoken as many times as necessary until you recognize the word *legislation* as it occurs in conversation.

$$\text{predominate} \quad \underset{1}{\underline{pr\breve{\imath}}} \quad \underset{2}{\underline{d\breve{o}m}} \quad \underset{3}{\underline{\partial}} \quad \underset{4}{\underline{n\bar{a}t}}$$

1. The *p* is formed with the lips natural; the *r* is a roll of the tongue; the short *i* is a narrow opening of the lips with the corners extended.

2. The *d* is made with the tongue to the palate; the short *o* is a medium opening of the lips; the *m* is made in the lips natural (closed) position.

3. The schwa *ə* has two sounds depending on if it occurs in the middle of a word or at the end of a word. This schwa *ə* sound is short and is made with a natural opening of the lips.

4. The *n* is made with the tongue to the palate; the long *a* by a medium opening with corners extended, followed by a quick, natural narrow movement; the *t* is made by touching the tongue to the palate.

Again, pronounce the word slowly, getting the feel of the word on the lips, tongue, and teeth, and noting the seen and unseen lip movements. Pronounce the word as naturally spoken until you are able to recognize *predominate* as a naturally spoken word.

6. Practice Techniques

Using the mirror system, you have learned the basic techniques of observing the lip movement of a word. Such observation is fundamental to lipreading, and you must master it in order to develop your skill. Later chapters will explain how to overcome the problem of interpreting unseen lip movements. You will learn to combine the techniques for seen and unseen movements so that you can understand words as they are spoken in conversation.

You will learn lipreading one word at a time. As you learn a word, use it in a short sentence to familiarize yourself with the way it looks in normal speech.

Now let's make short sentences containing the words you have learned so far. In each case, concentrate on the word you know. As you progress, you will begin to recognize the other words in the sentence. You will notice that, instead of knowing only one word in the sentence, you will begin to recognize two, three, or four words, until you can lipread the whole sentence.

sham

They fought a *sham* battle.

March

The month of *March* has thirty-one days.

fifth

He is the *fifth* person in line.

action

No *action* is necessary in this matter.

import

They paid 20 percent *import* duty.

phantom

"The *Phantom* of the Opera" is on TV tonight.

pamper

It is not wise to *pamper* a child too much.

automobile

The *automobile* was painted red.

condensation

Condensation was forming on the windowpanes.

legislation

The procedure was legalized by state *legislation*.

predominate

Which candidate will *predominate*?

Your main goal is to learn how the words you have studied look when spoken by other people. What you have learned by looking in the mirror must be applied to your conversations with others. Imagine that the mirror does not reflect you but reflects their image instead.

Make a list of the words and sentences you have studied. Ask a friend to seat himself about five to ten feet away and read them to you in a low voice. See how many words and sentences you can lipread on your friend's lips. If you grasp a few the first time, good work. Begin with sessions about five minutes long two to three times a week. In the meantime continue your mirror practice, adding new words and, most important, frequently reviewing what you have learned.

You must continue your mirror practice daily. Write on a small card a few words such as *lamp, small,* and *fall.* Every time you pass your mirror, stop long enough to review these words three or four times. Two or three times a week, change the words and practice new ones. Also write short sentences: (1) *What time is it?* (2) *Leave a note for him.* (3) *I will be home Wednesday.* Change your sentences after three or four days. After a few weeks have your helper read them to you to see how many you have mastered and can easily lipread.

When speaking, a person says a certain number of words per minute — usually one to three hundred. The average person who speaks well talks at a rate of approximately two hundred words per minute. Persons speaking at this moderate rate should have a clearly pronounced lip movement that can be grasped easily. Regardless, the lip movement will vary from person to person.

Persons speaking more than two hundred words per minute will have less lip movement, and their words will be more difficult to lipread. People who are rushed for time — fast-pitch salespersons and news commentators — usually speak at a greater number of words per minute than the average person.

As a general rule, any spoken word requires the same lip and tongue formations and the same expiration of air regardless of who is speaking. The only difference is in individual variations in speaking manner — whether a person speaks fast or slowly and whether he has an easily visible lip movement or just mumbles with little lip movement.

The following sections provide practice in lipreading spoken words. Enlist the help of another person — wife, husband, brother, sister, or friend — to help you.

7. Reading *b*, *m*, and *p*

The lips open from a closed position for *b* as in *bat*, *m* as in *mat*, *p* as in *pat*.

bat

Bat the ball.
The bat flew in through the window.
It's my turn to bat.

mat

Wipe your feet on the doormat.
The mat was two inches thick.
He had a heavy mat of hair.

pat

Give him a pat on the back.
I need a pat of butter.
She stood pat in her decision.

bake

Let's bake a cake.
You have to bake the bread for an hour.
I am going to bake a cake for the party.

mile

It's an even mile to the train station.
The next mile is downhill.
She walked a mile in eighteen minutes.

pick

The children went to pick apples at the farm.
Pick a bright color.
On your way home pick up a newspaper.

boat

Three people were in the rowboat.
The boat sank during the storm.
They went for a boat ride on the lake.

mark

The road has a white mark for each mile.
The store is going to mark down the price.
Put a check mark by the items needed.

pen

The pen is mightier than the sword.
Which pen will you use?
Each dog has its own pen at the kennel.

bond

His word was his bond.
We buy a saving bond every month.
The bond pays 6 percent interest.

model

She works as a model at the store.
They have a model of the new building on display.
The model was made of cardboard.

bill

We get a gas bill every month.
This is the fourth bill we sent.
The bird has a curved bill.

middle

They are a middle-aged couple.
You can't sit in the middle with only two chairs.
He was the middle-weight champion.

pine

It was a dense pine forest.
The candles have a pine scent.
The pine tree has long needles.

bone

The dishes were of bone china.
We are having T-bone steaks for supper.
She saves the ham bone to make soup.

burn

> The log will burn for hours.
> His curt reply made her burn with anger.
> The forest fire will burn for days.

mule

> He is as stubborn as a mule.
> Some farmers still use mules to plow.
> They went hunting for mule deer in the mountains.

8. Reading Short *a*

To form the short *a* as in *mat*, the lips open wide with the corners slightly drawn back and extended. The opening is the widest of the extended vowels.

anchor

> The big ship's anchor weighed a ton.
> Many an anchor has been lost at sea.
> The anchor held fast during the storm.

bank

> We bank at the town bank.
> The river bank was steep.
> Each of the children has a piggy bank.

can

> Anyone who wants to can go.
> Mother would can preserves every fall.
> We can ride the bus into town.

fancy

> She was footloose and fancy free.
> It strikes one's fancy.
> That store has some fancy prices.

hand

He worked as a farm hand last summer.
She always lends a helping hand to the needy.
The children get out of hand now and then.

hammer

I need some nails, a hammer, and ten minutes to work.
Give me a hammer and pliers.
You could hear the blacksmith hammer at the forge.

lamp

Leave the lamp by the window.
This oil lamp is an antique.
The miners use arc lamps.

latter

We are going the latter part of the week.
Mary will be over the latter part of the day.
We will pick the fruit the latter part of fall.

matter

It was a personal matter of concern to no one.
That is carrying matters too far.
Her opinion did not matter much.

narrow

Only a narrow-minded person thinks that way.
The bridge was too narrow for two-way traffic.
It was a narrow escape from drowning.

passage

We booked passage on the steamer to Europe.
A narrow passage led to the river.
The passage through the building was closed.

rapid

The rapid growth of the city was astounding.
The hikers set off at a rapid pace.
His rapid reply astounded me.

salmon

We intend to fish for salmon off the coast.
Salmon is very expensive these days.
I had a salmon salad for lunch today.

sand

The sun warmed the sand on the beach.
The children liked to play in the sand.
A rub with sandpaper removed the rust.

tap

Just tap on the window gently.
Not many taverns have beer on tap anymore.
Who would think they would tap telephone wires?

value

The price far exceeds the value.
Not many people value honor above riches.
Some people place little value on life.

9. Reading Short *e*

For short *e* as in *bet,* the opening of the lips is medium with a slight extension of the corners.

bend

Trees bend with the wind.
Don't bend your knees.
The plank will bend under all that weight.

cent

It cost a fraction of a cent to make.
Remember when a candy bar cost five cents?
The bank pays 4 percent interest.

desk

Paul sat at the small desk.
Move the desk toward the wall.
Use the desk in the library.

felt

We felt a cool breeze from the north.
She wore a felt hat today.
I felt sure he would join the club.

gentle

The dog has a gentle disposition.
Animals readily respond to gentle treatment.
A gentle wind came from the south.

length

The horse won by four lengths.
What is the length of your house?
A short length of pipe was needed.

melt

The hot sun would melt the tar on the roof.
We need a saucepan to melt the butter.
A small flame will melt the wax.

nest

The birds built a nest in the tree.
There are four birds in the nest.
The eggs in the nest are blue.

penny

A penny saved is a penny earned.
A penny for your thoughts.
He never earned an honest penny in his life.

rent

Our rent is due on the first.
The rent barely pays the landlord's expenses.
They want to rent under a long-term lease.

send

Send the package by parcel post.
It is quicker to send a telegram.
We intend to send our children to college.

vent

>One cannot vent one's wrath openly.
>The vent was closed in cold weather.
>The vent went through the roof.

well

>We have well water in our town.
>I knew him well.
>I wish I owned an oil well.

chest

>It was a small wooden chest.
>The ribs on the left side of the chest were broken.
>You will find the hammer in the tool chest.

dress

>Dress warmly; it is cold today.
>The children dress themselves now.
>She wore a dress of pure silk.

second

>He placed second in the race.
>I second the motion.
>The plane is due any second now.

10. Reading Short *i*

For the short *i* as in *sit*, the lip opening is narrow and the corners of the lips remain natural.

bill

>All bills are paid on the fifth.
>Our gas bill comes every two months.
>This is the third bill we forwarded.

bit

>We need a brace and bit to drill.
>Lift the plank a bit more.
>Every little bit counts.

dip

We took a dip in the pool before lunch.
Around the bend there is a dip in the road.
They dip it in tar to waterproof it.

fill

Have the druggist fill the prescription.
Please fill out this application.
Are there enough apples to fill the basket?

lift

We'll give you a lift home.
It is too heavy to lift alone.
Two men were needed to lift the anchor.

limit

A speed limit of 10 m.p.h. was posted.
They had a limit of two boxes per person.
The road extends beyond the city limits.

mint

He made a mint when he sold the stock.
The U.S. Mint is in Philadelphia.
The ice cream had a mint flavor.

mist

A heavy mist covered the swamp.
The mist blurred the setting sun.
It was a dreary day of mist and fog.

pill

Take one pill a day.
Remind me to take my pill at bedtime.
It was a bitter pill to swallow.

ring

Let him ring the bell.
Mary lost her wedding ring.
There were seven keys on the key ring.

shift

> He works on the night shift.
> The car has an automatic gear shift.
> A shift of wind brought cool air.

thick

> The walls were twelve inches thick.
> A thick forest of pines covered the valley.
> The dog has a thick coat of fur.

will

> He is a man of iron will.
> They will be home this week end.
> Who will go to the store?

visit

> We are going to visit my aunt.
> John's family will visit us in May.
> Our uncle will visit us next week.

silver

> She wore a silver fox cape.
> They will celebrate their silver anniversary.
> No silver coins are minted anymore.

11. Reading Short *o*

For the sound of short *o* as in *hot,* the lips remain natural and the opening is medium.

bond

> His word was his bond.
> The deed was written on bond paper.
> First prize was a government bond.

dollar

> The price was a dollar each.
> He has a silver dollar issued in 1898.
> Whose picture is on the five-dollar bill?

follow

> Just follow the path to the brook.
> You go ahead; I'll follow later.
> Follow instructions closely.

box

> Put the present in a box.
> His father taught him to box.
> Try not to box him in.

hollow

> It had a hollow sound when tapped.
> They live in the hollow by the forest.
> The bomb exploded with a hollow roar.

knock

> Please knock before you enter.
> He won by a knockout in the third round.
> Water in the gas caused a knock in the motor.

model

> A clay model was made first.
> He builds model airplanes for a pastime.
> She works as a model in the store.

polish

> We need a can of shoe polish.
> It took all day to polish the silver.
> The children will polish the furniture.

solid

> She wore a ring of solid gold.
> We had to stand for three solid hours.
> A table of solid oak filled the room.

dock

> He was docked one hour's pay.
> The boat is in dry dock for repairs.
> At what pier will the boat dock?

follow

> I fail to follow his thinking.
> You go on ahead and I will follow later.
> The children are playing follow the leader.

plot

> He intends to plot the ship's course.
> The land was divided into half-acre plots.
> Can you think of a good plot for a story?

lock

> The police had to lock him in a cell.
> When you leave, please lock the door.
> He bought the store, lock, stock, and barrel.

modest

> She is a very modest person.
> We own a modest home on the edge of town.
> Choose any modest, self-respecting person.

hot

> The weather is hot and humid today.
> A hot temper is not an asset.
> Is there enough hot water for a bath?

proper

> When is the proper time to plant corn?
> The west wall would be the proper place for the stove.
> Would it be proper to phone him?

12. Reading *f* and *v*

To form *f* or *v*, as in *face* or *vase,* the lower lip touchs the upper teeth.

favor

> The voters did not favor the bond issue.
> She is hoping for a favorable answer.
> Mother favored Tom more than the other boys.

fall

    We expect a good harvest this fall.
    We had a two-inch snowfall last night.
    On these cool nights you need a fall coat.

feed

    Ask the tall fellow in the feed store.
    Is there enough hay to feed the horse?
    She had enough food to feed an army.

fly

    Birds fly south in the fall.
    We intend to fly to Europe next month.
    Who would think man would fly into outer space?

frost

    Mary has to frost the cake before we go.
    The weatherman predicts frost tonight.
    A heavy frost covered the ground.

vote

    We vote for a new president next year.
    A majority vote was needed.
    You can vote from 6 A.M. till 6 P.M.

vase

    A large vase held the roses.
    She collects antique vases.
    A hand-painted vase was on the table.

foot

    Why don't you make it a foot longer?
    The step was a foot high.
    Who intends to foot the bill for this project?

view

    In view of the circumstances it had to be done.
    From the mountain you have a view of the entire valley.
    You have a nice view from your window.

fine

> The coin contains one ounce of fine silver.
> He was fined $10.00 for speeding.
> Everything's fine and dandy at our house.

left

> Turn left at the next corner.
> Mary left without saying goodbye.
> I left my umbrella on the train again.

voice

> He voiced his opinions freely.
> Tom's voice was harsh due to a cold.
> I didn't recognize your voice on the phone.

full

> A full report of the accident was needed.
> There will be a full moon Friday.
> The bushel basket was full of apples.

velvet

> She wore a black velvet dress.
> Most jewel boxes are lined with velvet.
> He seems to have that velvet touch.

fire

> The forest fire burned for days.
> A warm, cozy fire was burning in the fireplace.
> Report all fires to the fire department.

13. Reading Short *u*

For short *u* as in *fun,* the opening of the lips is medium and the lips remain natural. Short *o* and short *u* are almost identical in lip movement with some words falling in the category of homophonous words: *pomp-pump, hot-hut, lock-luck, sock-suck, son-sun, some-sum.*

but

> No one but you heard the story.
> No ifs, ands, or buts — do it.
> I'll have a slice of beef, but not too much.

butter

> I'd like one pound of butter, please.
> We don't care much for apple butter at our house.
> Have a peanut-butter-and-jelly sandwich.

dust

> That joke was so old it had dust on it.
> A cloud of dust covered the field.
> We watched the miners pan for gold dust.

fund

> The pension fund was in bonds.
> We provided a fund to pay the interest.
> The money was placed in a fund for later use.

husky

> It takes a husky person to farm.
> He speaks with a husky voice.
> The sled was pulled by four husky dogs.

dull

> The day was dull and dreary.
> His speech was long and rather dull.
> You can't cut wood with a dull axe.

trust

> The money was in a trust fund.
> Mail the bill to the Peoples Bank & Trust Company.
> Is he a person you can trust?

sun

> The sunlight filtered through the trees.
> We watched the sun set last night.
> It was a hot, blazing sun in a cloudless sky.

lunch

 The lunch hour is from twelve to one.
 Meet me for lunch tomorrow.
 The children take their lunch to school.

pump

 An electric pump was installed last week.
 New pumps were installed at the gas station.
 Grandpa's farm still has the old hand pump.

supply

 We need a supply of paper.
 Who can supply all these items?
 The supply of sugar exceeded the demand.

gum

 May I have a pack of chewing gum?
 For class bring a pencil and artgum eraser.
 All children chew bubble gum.

hunch

 Have you read *The Hunchback of Notre Dame*?
 I have a hunch this horse will win.
 On cold days we hunched over the campfire.

thumb

 To save bus fare he thumbed his way home.
 I'm all thumbs when it comes to sewing.
 As usual he missed the nail and hit his thumb.

son

 My son went to the beach for a sunbath.
 Her son graduates this year.
 His oldest son is studying to be a doctor.

wonder

 I wonder if the story is true.
 We wonder why she left.
 We walk through the forest and wonder about our problem.

some

It must be some place in this room.
Some unknown person donated $100.
Put some flowers in the vase.

color

Use a deep blue color.
What color shall we paint the bedroom?
The right color scheme will be needed.

touch

It seems everybody will touch wet paint.
He had a touch of sarcasm in his voice.
The soup needs a touch of salt.

14. Reading Broad *a*

For the sound of a broad *a* (*ah*), the lips remain natural with the lip
opening the widest of all the relaxed vowels.

alarm

Set the alarm clock for seven.
The building has a burglar alarm system.
The news is no cause for alarm.

bark

The dog was trained to bark at strangers.
Birch bark has a sweet smell.
The bark of the tree was stripped by lightning.

car

The neighbors own three cars.
Our firm leases their cars.
His car is hard to start in cold weather.

dark

He wore a dark suit to the meeting.
Dark brown would be a better color.
It was a dark and dreary day.

farm

> We have a small farm out west.
> The farm house will be painted tomorrow.
> He has the largest farm in the state.

guard

> Trained dogs guard the plant at night.
> Armed guards protected the shipment of gold.
> Father is an armed guard at the bank.

jar

> Put the flowers in the glass jar.
> Bring home a jar of pickles.
> Mother canned 59 jars of peaches.

mark

> On your mark, get set, go!
> They did not mark the price down.
> Just mark the items needed.

march

> The first payment was due March first.
> The troops march at dawn.
> It was Tuesday, March the tenth.

park

> The park is crowded today.
> Will you park the car for me?
> The ballpark was half empty.

part

> They found the missing part three days later.
> Part your hair on the left side.
> Romeo, to part is such sweet sorrow.

scarf

> Wear a silk scarf tonight.
> In cold weather a wool scarf helps.
> Wear a bright scarf with the dress.

harm

Will the wax harm the paint?
It can do no harm to try.
The mugger intended to do him bodily harm.

what

What time shall I meet you?
What reason did he give?
I really don't know what happened.

garage

We painted the garage last week.
The house has a two-car garage.
During winter, we store the boat in the garage.

15. Reading *d, n,* and *t*

For *d, n,* and *t* the flat edge of the tongue touches the palate and the teeth are close together. This tongue movement is difficult to see.

treat

On halloween it's trick or treat.
Thursday is my time to treat for lunch.
The doctor prescribed medical treatment for her.

neat

Her home is always neat as a pin.
We made a neat profit on that deal.
Her typing was neatly done.

date

When you're at the store get some dates and nuts.
We have a date for dinner Thursday.
Be sure to date the check correctly.

direct

Can you direct me to the post office?
What was the direct result of the meeting?
Mr. Jones will direct the orchestra tonight.

dust

  Mabel will dust the furniture today.
  A dusty road led to the farm.
  That region has been a dust bowl for years.

need

  We will need to know the truth of the matter.
  There is no need to get upset about the affair.
  They need more help at the factory.

new

  I hope the new year will be better for us.
  After seven years I think we need a new car.
  The new moon will be on the twenty-third this month.

nut

  Fasten the board with a nut and bolt.
  Mother made a date and nut cake for the party.
  That's the entire story in a nutshell.

take

  Have John take a snapshot of the waterfall.
  It's my job to take the dog for a walk.
  Miss Jones will take your phone order.

tent

  The scouts slept in a pup tent.
  For a while the workers lived in a tent.
  Our tent sleeps six persons.

down

  It was downhill all the way.
  We prefer down pillows at our house.
  Sales were down for the last quarter.

total

  What is the total of sales for today?
  Carry a subtotal for each page.
  The project was a total failure.

name

A name and date are needed on line one.
Sign your name on the bottom.
May I have your name and phone number?

nine

Nine persons rode the bus.
He will be nineteen tomorrow.
The new store hours are from nine to nine.

tool

Keep the mower in the toolshed.
He works at the tool and die shop on the corner.
Bring your own tools.

16. Reading Long *e*

For the long *e* as in *beet,* the lip opening is narrow and the lips extend at the corners.

beet

We had beets for supper last night.
He turned red as a beet when she answered.
Fresh beets are on the market now.

cheap

He is selling cheap merchandise now.
You can buy them cheaper by the dozen.
He is feeling cheap at his mistake.

beech

A small beech tree was planted in the park.
You don't see many beech trees around here.
Are beechnuts edible?

week

A work week is forty hours.
It has rained for a week.
Why not spend the weekend at our house.

seam

Sew a double seam at the waist.
The suit needs resewing at the seam.
You will have to sew the seam by hand.

lean

He seems to lean toward socialism.
The post leans towards the west.
Get some lean beef for stew at the butcher's.

see

You can see for miles from the mountain.
Most people see much but remember little.
I will see you next Tuesday.

green

The green timber was hard to ignite.
The grass is turning green.
We will have to pick the green beans soon.

deep

Take a deep breath before you dive.
He seems to be absorbed in deep thought.
The pool was five feet deep.

fear

She has a fear of snakes.
He has no fear he will lose his money.
The child fears the neighbor's dog.

meet

We will meet at 5th and Main streets.
Have John meet me at the airport.
We intend to meet the governor at the banquet.

need

> I don't see any need to apologize.
> We will need more money for gas.
> We need new tires for the car.

preach

> Practice what you preach.
> The pastor is too ill to preach this Sunday.
> More people should practice what they preach.

season

> The baseball season just started.
> This summer was a dull season in trade.
> The hunting season starts in October.

sea

> A calm sea made swimming enjoyable.
> The seabirds followed the ship for days.
> The land is five feet above sea level.

17. Reading Short *oo*

For the short *oo* as in *look,* the lip opening is medium and the lips pucker and thrust forward slightly.

book

> Put your book in the desk.
> Have you read a good book lately?
> I left my book on the train.

brook

> The water in the brook is cold.
> A small brook runs through our property.
> Mountain snows feed the brook.

cook

> I cook three meals a day.
> Our cook is ill today.
> I'll tell the cook to prepare supper.

good

> Have a good time on your vacation.
> He has a good credit rating.
> Today should be a good day for fishing.

hook

> Hang your coat on the lower hook.
> She's making a hooked rug for the hall.
> He gets what he wants by hook or by crook.

hood

> You can see Mount Hood from our home.
> We need a hood over our stove.
> I prefer a winter jacket with a hood.

foot

> My left foot is larger than my right foot.
> I need a board a foot wide.
> He tries to put his best foot forward.

look

> I'll have to look for a larger home.
> Look before you cross the street.
> Don't look yet.

poor

> The soil is too poor for farming.
> She has been in poor health lately.
> Unless we get rain soon we will have a poor wheat crop.

wood

> The whiskey was aged in wood nine years.
> A wood crate held the children's toys.
> We need a supply of wood for the fireplace.

wool

> Take your wool sweater with you.
> I have a heavy wool coat for winter.
> The store features woolen clothing from Scotland.

push

> We are pushed for time.
> I had to push my way through the crowd.
> They had to push the car to the garage.

bush

> Plant the rose bush in the corner of the yard.
> We have too many bushes now.
> Don't beat around the bush if you know the answer.

18. Reading Long *oo*

The long *oo* as in *broom,* the long *u* as in *flute,* and the long *u* as in *human* (see Chapter 19) have homophonous lip movement; the lips pucker and thrust forward with a narrow opening.

boost

> They are trying to boost their sales.
> The bonus gave a big boost to employee morale.
> This is the second boost in milk prices in a month.

broom

> A new broom sweeps clean.
> We need a new whisk broom.
> You'll find the broom in the hall closet.

cool

> He remained cool, calm, and collected during the argument.
> Any cool drink is welcome on a hot day.
> The cool fall evenings were enjoyable.

food

> His idea was food for thought.
> The tornado caused a food shortage in the town.
> A supply of canned foods was kept for emergencies.

groom

The children were well groomed for the party.
He's in the barn grooming the horses.
The animals were groomed daily for the show.

spool

I need a spool of black thread.
The wire is wound on a metal spool.
You will use more than one spool of thread.

loose

Wind the yarn loosely in a ball.
Some shingles became loose in the storm.
Tie your shoelace a little looser.

moon

We will have a full moon tonight.
Plant your crops on the increasing moon.
We would sit on the beach and watch the moon rise.

noon

Let's try to finish our work before noon.
Meet me for lunch at noon today.
The plant closes at noon on Saturday.

pool

Shall we take a dip in the pool before lunch?
The men are playing pool in the basement.
Four of us are in the car pool now.

proof

The document will have to be proofread.
That brand of whiskey is 90 proof.
He lacked proof that the document was signed by Jones.

root

Root beer is my favorite drink.
They say money is the root of all evil.
I guess I rooted for the wrong team.

tool

> He works in the tool and die shop on the corner.
> The mechanics have to furnish their own tools.
> The purse was hand tooled leather.

roof

> The roof is in need of repair.
> His roof was damaged during the storm.
> My kite landed on the roof.

19. Reading Long *u*

For long *u* as in *fuse*, the lips pucker with a narrow opening. The long *u* sound can also be spelled *ew* as in *few* and *ue* as in *hue*.

cube

> Put in some ice cubes to cool the water.
> The coin was set in a plastic cube.
> Have the butcher cut the meat in cubes.

argue

> It's useless to argue with him.
> I will argue against the proposed law.
> The panel argued for a just cause.

human

> To err is human; to forgive divine.
> No other human being would want his job.
> The dog was almost human.

fuse

> This is the last good electric fuse we have.
> For safety, the fuse should be ten feet long.
> The metals will not fuse below eight hundred degrees.

future

> They are planning to move south in the near future.
> What will happen in the future is hard to tell.
> The company purchased the land for future use.

huge

> She has a huge collection of antiques stored in the barn.
> We will need a huge hall for the convention.
> A huge crowd gathered for the event.

mule

> He still uses a team of mules to plow the field.
> This forest abounds with mule deer.
> The mine still uses mules to haul supplies.

music

> She takes her music lessons on Thursday.
> He cannot read a note of music, but he can play a guitar.
> Who wrote the music score for the play?

pupil

> He is a pupil in Mr. Smith's class.
> The doctor dilated the pupil of the boy's eye.
> Not many pupils attended the lecture.

cue

> A door slam was his cue to enter.
> Each line of dialogue is a cue for an actor.
> The billiard cue was warped.

union

> He is a member of the carpenter's union.
> I misplaced my union card.
> The factory has been a union shop for years.

hue

> All the hues of the rainbow were seen.
> His painting was in pale hues.
> Heed the hue and cry of the voters.

use

> This old lumber is of no practical use.
> May I use your car for a while?
> He won't let anybody use his tools.

usual

> This is our usual July weather.
> I usually walk to the train.
> More people than usual were on the bus.

When long *u* takes the pronunciation of long *oo* the lip movement is identical to long *u* that has the *ew* sound.

blue

> Wear the dark blue suit.
> The sky was clear blue today.
> The room was blue from smoke.

crude

> The price of crude oil increased again.
> I didn't expect a crude answer.
> The tanker held crude oil.

fruit

> We had fruit salad for dessert.
> The fruit is in the refrigerator.
> Order a fruitcake from the market.

June

> She was married in the month of June.
> June and July are warm months.
> His vacation will be in June this year.

prune

> I have to prune the bushes soon.
> They usually have prunes for breakfast.
> Once in a while we have prune coffeecake.

spruce

> I would like to spruce up before we leave.
> Norway spruce lined the road.
> We have a blue spruce in the yard.

truth

    He swore to tell the truth.
    I question the truth of that statement.
    I doubt the truth of her story.

20. Reading *aw* and *o* as in *or*

For the *aw* as in *raw* and the *o* as in *or,* the lips pucker slightly, with a wide opening. The opening is the widest of puckered vowels.

tall

    Tall trees shaded the house.
    Tom is tall for his age.
    The tall tree is a sugar maple.

raw

    They use the barn to store raw materials.
    I prefer raw carrots.
    The boat carried a shipment of raw sugar.

north

    Our house is on the north side of town.
    It was too cloudy to see the North Star.
    My uncle lives in the northern part of Ohio.

saw

    I have to saw an inch off the board.
    Take this saw to be sharpened.
    A power saw saves a lot of work.

border

    We should reach the Canadian border in an hour.
    We have a border of flagstones around the garden.
    Her notepaper has a dark blue border.

dawn

    The boat sails at dawn.
    The idea dawned on him too late.
    During winter the newspapers are delivered before dawn.

order

    The book was ordered last week.

    Our phone is out of order.

    I have to have my shoes made to order.

call

    Let me call you back in a few minutes.

    This occasion calls for a cool head.

    I must call the dentist for an appointment.

lawn

    Our lawn is mowed every week.

    Mabel intends to wear her blue dress to the lawn party.

    The lawn mower needs sharpening.

short

    Mary stopped by for a short visit.

    She wants a blouse with short sleeves.

    Take a shortcut through the prairie.

caught

    I finally caught up on my work.

    He caught the ball with his left hand.

    The police caught John shooting ducks out of season.

fall

    He can fall asleep anytime.

    Christmas falls on a Monday this year.

    We had a heavy rainfall this summer.

orange

    She wore an orange blouse.

    Our orange trees are heavy with fruit.

    We prefer orange pekoe tea at our house.

haul

    They had to haul the logs from the forest.

    We will need a larger truck to haul that size load.

    He operates a short haul truck company.

order

> Shall we order our meal now?
> We placed our order by phone.
> He followed the sergeant's orders.

for

> Apples are priced three pounds for a dollar.
> I have an engagement for the evening.
> He is tall for his age.

21. Reading Long *a* (Diphthong)

The long *a* as in *bale* is a double movement. The lip opening is medium with the corners extended, followed by a quick, relaxed, narrow movement.

lane

> A narrow lane led to the brook.
> It's a two-lane highway all the way.
> The accident blocked both lanes of traffic.

base

> It was a three-base hit.
> The statue stood on a marble base.
> John's a true baseball fan.

grade

> A good grade of paper was needed.
> Tom is in third grade at school.
> She will grade the test papers tomorrow.

daily

> The newspaper was delivered daily.
> He would walk to work daily.
> Factory help was paid a daily wage.

face

Our new house will face north.

Most flowers face the sun.

We must face the facts on this issue.

late

The hour was late when we returned.

As usual she is late.

We always watch the late news on TV.

mail

Any mail today?

Mail it today.

We received our tax bill in the mail last week.

name

Write down your name and phone number.

You name the day you want to go.

The face I remember; the name I forget.

paint

We will paint our house next week.

The sign said: Wet paint; do not touch.

What color shall we paint the living room?

paste

We need some toothpaste.

Paste the pictures in the album.

Only paste the edges of the paper.

rain

Save a little for a rainy day.

A steady rain fell for hours.

The weatherman predicts rain for today.

sale

Johnson's house is for sale.

Every item is marked down 20 percent during our fall sale.

Over a hundred homes were listed for sale.

stain

    The stain could not be removed.

    Stain the wood a dark brown.

    She could not remove the stain from her dress.

train

    The train was four minutes late.

    The last train makes all stops.

    They will train the dog for show purposes.

waste

    Waste nothing; want nothing.

    His speech was a waste of time.

    Empty the wastebasket.

22. Reading Long *i* (Diphthong)

For long *i,* as in *pipe,* the lips remain natural with a wide opening followed by a quick narrow movement.

bite

    Don't bite off more than you can chew.

    At that lake the mosquitoes bite more than the fish.

    A barking dog seldom bites.

dime

    Stop at the dime store for thread.

    Do you have change for a dime?

    His ideas are a dime a dozen.

fire

    Where there is smoke there is fire.

    He worked in the fire department garage.

    A warm fire burned in the fireplace.

hide

    The children played hide and seek all evening.

    He wanted a horsehide belt.

    She tried to hide the facts.

life

Tom was the life of the party.
The ship had only one lifeboat.
We need more lifeguards at the pool.

side

Please sit on the other side.
They tried to sidestep the issue.
Place the vase on the left side.

wire

They need a barbed wire fence for the cattle.
Our office has direct wire service to New York.
The robbers cut the phone wires.

vine

They lived in a vine-covered cottage.
Grapevines grew wild in the valley.
Ivy vines shaded the porch.

shine

The sunshine warmed the valley.
I have to shine my shoes.
We have to shine the silver before the party.

mile

The scouts went on a ten-mile hike.
The lake is three miles long and a mile wide.
We average sixteen miles to the gallon.

light

The light burned all night.
His camera has a built-in light meter.
The town installed a stoplight at the intersection.

pipe

Our furnace pipe is old and rusty.
The gas pipe was installed underground.
Our water pipes froze in the cold spell.

night

>It rained all night last night.
>We keep a night light burning in the hall.
>John works nights at the factory.

chime

>The clock only chimes the hour.
>Our door chime is not working.
>The church bell chimes only on Sunday.

23. Reading Long *o* (Diphthong)

For the long *o* as in *sole,* the lips make a double movement. First the opening is wide with a slight pucker; then the lips become still more puckered.

blow

>He gave a blow-by-blow description of the fight.
>We had a blowout on the way home.
>It's cool when the wind blows from the north.

bone

>Give the dog a bone.
>Oh boy! I sure pulled a boner that time.
>Add a soup bone for more flavor.

both

>Both of my boys are in school.
>Place both arms overhead.
>Both players are over six feet tall.

broke

>Let's go for broke.
>She left with a broken heart.
>Borrow from John; I'm broke this week.

cold

>Baby, it's cold outside.
>They live in a cold climate.
>I have had this cold for over a week.

flow

Water never flows uphill.
A small river flows through the valley.
The tar would not flow through the pipe.

horse

As usual my horse came in last.
She rode a palomino horse in the parade.
Don't put the cart before the horse.

alone

She lives alone in the white house.
Mother told me never to walk home alone.
I went alone to the meeting.

over

Don't pay over a hundred for it.
Don't let the coffee boil over.
Put a cover over the lumber to protect it from the rain.

road

The state road needs repaving.
They live on the country road outside of town.
A steep and narrow road leads to the farm.

rode

Through the valley the cavalry rode.
She rode a horse in the parade.
The children rode in the back of the truck.

shore

A deserted cabin stood on the seashore.
We beached our boat on the shore during the storm.
She picked sea shells on the seashore.

24. Reading *ow* (Diphthong)

The *ow* as in *brown* is a double movement. First, the lip opening is wide, lip corners natural, followed by a more puckered movement, with lips continuing to thrust forward. The same movement is made for *ou* when it has the *ow* sound as in *loud*.

brown

> Wear the brown hat and shoes.
> Brown the meat in a skillet before adding the vegetables.
> They live in the brownstone house on the hill.

town

> The next town is fifty miles away.
> Their store is on the town square.
> Does anybody know the population of our town?

frown

> His frown showed his displeasure at the project.
> Her frown turned to a smile of approval.
> He's had a frown on his face all day.

brow

> He earns his money by the sweat of his brow.
> His tanned brow showed he worked outdoors.
> She had a cute way of arching her eyebrow.

down

> I prefer to sleep on down pillows.
> Make a small down payment; pay the balance in ninety days.
> Miss Jones will take down the minutes of the meeting.

power

> Our car has power brakes and power steering.
> The power lines were blown down during the storm.
> Most factories use electric power today.

plow

> Our field was plowed last week.
> The village had three snowplows working during the storm.
> The heavy rains prevented the farmers from plowing the fields.

tower

> The observation tower was six hundred feet high.
> A forest of towering pines filled the valley.
> Sears Tower is the world's tallest building.

owl

The railroad runs an "owl" train for theatergoers.
The owl roosts on that top rafter.
There are three owlets in the owl roost.

towel

The maid put clean towels in the bathroom.
Spread a beach towel to sit on.
The dish towels are in the lower cabinet.

powder

I have to stop at the drugstore for face powder.
The gunpowder is stored in a separate building.
The old car isn't worth the powder to blow it up.

pound

Get two pounds of steak from the butcher.
We're having pound cake for dessert tonight.
The rice comes only in two-pound packages.

cloud

Since her engagement she's been on cloud nine.
It was a warm day with no clouds in the sky.
Most of the city was flooded from the cloudburst.

flower

We have more weeds than flowers.
My niece will be the flower girl at the wedding.
Use a clay flower pot.

flour

Add two cups of flour and three eggs.
Mrs. Jones, may I borrow a cup of flour?
We prefer bread that has some whole-wheat flour.

ground

The ground was barren from the drought.
New playground equipment is being installed.
Murphy hit a grounder to first base.

loud

    He gave his speech in a loud, clear voice.

    That radio has three loudspreakers.

    I couldn't hear you, as the radio was on too loud.

mount

    You can see Mount McKinley in the distance.

    Mount the pictures on the wall.

    He is a member of the Royal Canadian Mounted Police.

round

    Give me the total in round figures.

    The soldiers were issued ten rounds of ammunition.

    The ranchers were preparing for the annual roundup.

south

    Our house is on the south side of the street.

    We will go south for the holidays.

    A warm south wind heralds the coming of spring.

crowd

    A large crowd watched the parade.

    A jolly crowd attended the dance.

    On warm days the beach is usually crowded.

25. Reading *oy* (Diphthong)

The *oy* is a double movement. The lips pucker with a wide opening followed by a quick, natural, narrow opening.

boy

    Our family has three boys and one girl.

    The boy across the street mows our lawn.

    John will join the Boy Scouts next month.

enjoy

    I enjoy an evening walk in the park.

    Everybody enjoyed the concert last night.

    We spent an enjoyable evening at the Martins'.

oil

    I put a quart of oil in the car.
She owns an oil painting by Van Gogh.
Oil the hinges on the door.

boil

    Boil my eggs for three minutes.
Let the soup boil for an hour.
He has a painful boil on his arm.

foil

    A pair of fencing foils hung on the wall.
Wrap the meat in aluminum foil.
The ceiling was covered with tinfoil to keep out the heat.

moist

    The ground was moist from the morning dew.
That fern needs a moist climate to grow properly.
The moist air foretold of the coming rains.

join

    Let's join the folks in the living room.
Just join the two ends together.
Bert's son joined the Boy Scouts last week.

noise

    The noise in the factory is unbearable.
Don't make more noise than necessary.
It is a soundproof room to keep out the noise.

point

    I'll have to sharpen the point on this pencil.
He missed the main point of the story.
I hesitated to point out his error.

spoil

    Spare the rod and spoil the child.
Food spoils quickly in this warm weather.
Too much salt will spoil the taste of the salad.

toy

> He is toying with the idea of building a boat.
> The toy was broken when it was dropped.
> We are collecting toys for the orphanage.

void

> The room was void of furniture.
> We are trying to have the contract voided.
> I don't know why the bank voided the check.

voice

> You must speak in a loud, clear voice to be heard.
> Does anybody care to voice an opinion on the subject?
> Her voice was so low you could hardly hear her.

coil

> The rattlesnake was coiled to strike.
> The rope was coiled in hundred-foot lengths.
> That's the last coil of wire I have.

coin

> I save silver coins as a hobby.
> The date on the coin was 1898.
> His collection of coins is very valuable.

26. Reading Compound Words

One great advantage for the lipreader is the fact that English has many compound words. Look at the following five words: (1) foot, (2) base, (3) ball, (4) hand, (5) volley. If you master these, you might say that you have learned to lipread five words. In reality, however, you have learned nine words, including four compounds: (1) foot, (2) base, (3) ball, (4) hand, (5) volley, (6) football, (7) baseball, (8) handball, (9) volleyball.

After you have mastered two words *base* and *ball,* it is simple to turn them into one word, *baseball.*

for

The money will be used for a new school.

give

Give me a good reason for not going.

forgive

It is not easy to forgive a wrong.

under

The ball rolled under the auto.

stand

We had to stand in line for an hour.

understand

I did not understand the question.

day

It was a warm day in June.

break

Plastic dishes won't break when you drop them.

daybreak

They left at daybreak to go fishing.

end

Her room is at the end of the hall.

less

This one weighs less than the other one.

endless

It was an endless wait in line for tickets.

every

She was given every opportunity to succeed.

one

Only one person could go.

everyone

Everyone has his own idea.

fire

The forest fire burned for days.

wood

The chest was made of wood.

firewood

Old logs were used for firewood.

horse
  As usual, my horse finished last in the race.
back
  Please bring the book back by Saturday.
horseback
  They went horseback riding this evening.

long
  We need a board three feet long.
hand
  Will you hand me the hammer?
longhand
  The note was written in longhand.

main
  A horse race was the main attraction at the fair.
land
  He owns some land in the valley.
mainland
  The ship was fifty miles from the mainland.

pass
  Pass on the right side.
book
  Read a good book.
passbook
  I will need my passbook today.

tea
  Do you prefer tea or coffee?
spoon
  One spoon of sugar, please.
teaspoon
  It was a pewter teaspoon.

ring
  Did you hear the telephone ring?
side
  Sit on the left side.
ringside
  We had ringside seats for the boxing match.

---

27. Reading *l*

For *l* as in *lend,* the point of the tongue touches the palate. The movement may be visible after the enunciation of the *l,* just before the sound of vowel that follows.

land

> The plane will land on the east runway.
> The landlord came for the rent.
> It took him an hour to land the fish.

late

> We arrived late for the meeting.
> Let's not go at this late hour.
> John's plane will be an hour late.

left

> She left the meeting early.
> Sit on the left side.
> Make a left turn at the next corner.

leap

> Look before you leap.
> Next year will be leap year.
> The children played leapfrog all morning.

line

> He hit a line drive to left field.
> They are installing a new gas line in our town.
> She had a jewel box lined in velvet.

little

> Give me a little more time.
> I like the little white dog.
> Ours is the little house on the corner.

fall

> The fall air was cool and crisp.
> Oh to be young and fall in love again.
> It was the first snowfall of the year.

loose

>Hold the loose end of the rope.
>A loose wire caused the short circuit.
>I must see the dentist about this loose tooth.

long

>How long will they stay down south?
>The pastor gave a long sermon this morning.
>Bring a long piece of rope.

look

>Will you help me look for my keys?
>Look up his number in the phone book.
>We want to look for a new home.

load

>That's too heavy a load for you to carry.
>It takes him an hour to load his truck.
>The truck could carry only a five-ton load.

lock

>Be sure to lock the door when you leave.
>We watched the ships go through the locks.
>For security they have double locks on the doors.

luck

>He seems to have good luck in any venture.
>I always carry a lucky penny.
>Perhaps lady luck will smile your way.

28. Reading *r*

The lips pucker or draw in at the corners to form an *r* before a vowel, as in *reel.* After a vowel, as in *urn,* little or no movement is shown, for the *r* tends to be slurred. In *charm, firm* and *form,* the only noticeable movement is a very slight delay between the vowel and the final consonant.

rain

The weatherman predicted rain for today.
A heavy rain flooded the valley.
It rained for five days in a row.

rate

What is the tax rate in our town?
What rate of interest is to be charged?
The legal rate of interest is high in our state.

real

He works in the real estate office.
Charles is a real image of his father.
His real estate was placed in a trust.

rest

He says there's no rest for the wicked.
Store the rest of the apples in the barn.
Let's rest for a few moments.

room

We rent a three-room apartment.
Fourteen people sat in the dining room.
Our house has three rooms on the first floor.

reply

No reply is necessary.
The firm has not replied to my letter.
This is our third letter without a reply.

roll

Rock and roll music is all you hear these days.
Her hobby is collecting music rolls.
Have a roll call taken to check the members present.

right

Sit on the right side of the table.
Turn to the right at the next crossing.
She left for home right after lunch.

ring

Did the doorbell ring?
She misplaced her wedding ring.
The key ring held four keys.

round

The soldiers were issued ten rounds of ammunition.
What is the total in round figures?
We played two rounds of golf.

rush

He is always in a rush.
Rush orders were issued to the troops.
Bus service slows up during the rush hours.

road

Which road will we take?
They are paving the road.
It's a paved road all the way.

read

I read one book a month.
She was unable to read his writing.
Tom reads the newspaper on the train.

run

Walk, do not run, to the nearest exit.
They built a run for their dog.
We had to run to catch the train.

rope

We watched the cowboys rope cattle.
A heavier rope will be needed.
We always carry a tow rope in the car.

burn

He was burning with anger.
The charcoal will burn for hours.
It's against the law to burn leaves.

farm

    Stop at the farm for vegetables.
He's been a farmer all his life.
We only grow wheat on our farm.

29. Reading Homophonous Words

    Homophonous words are words that when spoken take identical lip movements although the spelling and meaning are not the same. Take, for example, the following words: (1) shade and jade, (2) pail, mail, male, and bail, (3) beat and meat. When spoken these words have identical lip movement. However, the meanings and spellings are different.

shade, jade

    We need a shade for the west window.
Sit in the shade; it's a little cooler there.

    The jade statue came from China.
Jane wants jade earrings for her birthday.

pail, mail, male, bail

    The milk pail is in the barn.
The wooden pail came from the farm.

    The mail is late today.
Send this letter by air mail.

    We found a male collie last night that was lost.
Our church has an all male choir.

    They have to bail the water from the boat.
We had to post bail for speeding.

beat, meat

    No one beats a rug anymore.
John beat me by four games.

    We don't eat meat on Friday.
We store our meat in a freezer.

30. Reading *th*

To form *th,* the tongue touches the upper teeth.

thaw

> The ice on the river is beginning to thaw.
> Thaw out the freezer chest.
> The sun will thaw the icicles on the trees.

thin

> The board is too thin to hold that weight.
> How thin shall I slice the bread?
> The paint is too thin to cover in one coat.

third

> Jack placed third in the swimming race.
> That's the third time the phone has rung this morning.
> Our office is on the third floor.

throw

> The children like to throw stones in the lake.
> Don't throw these old papers away.
> We need a throw rug in the living room.

with

> I'll have coffee with sugar and milk.
> The board was painted with black paint.
> Bring your golf clubs with you on your vacation.

length

> This horse won by a length and a half.
> The length of our lot is one hundred feet.
> Deliver four lengths of one-inch pipe to Mr. Jones.

thick

> I think the cake batter is too thick.
> These oranges have a thick skin.
> The castle walls are two feet thick.

width

Is the width greater than the length?
What width is this dress material?
Measure the length and width of the barn.

thumb

To save money they thumbed a ride home.
He hit his thumb with the hammer.
They say Mr. Timms has a green thumb.

moth

The clothes were packed with mothballs.
They say an amber light doesn't attract moths.
We don't have many moths in our climate.

health

Let's drink to your health.
Tom has always been a healthy person.
Sarah has been in poor health lately.

cloth

Use a clean tablecloth tonight.
The washcloths are three for a dollar.
The brown cloth is too dark to match the shoes.

three

Only three people attended the meeting.
We need three more chairs.
Our area code is three-two-three.

south

We intend to go south for the winter.
Their home is on the south side of the street.
Most birds fly south in September.

thread

Will someone thread this needle for me?
I need a spool of black thread.
We had to thread our way through the crowds.

than
> John is much older than Mary.
> The forum required an adult other than their parents.
> I think the blue coat is better than the brown.

that
> Mabel said that she would be here tonight.
> This is an oak tree; that one is a maple.
> I would rather take this coat than that one.

the
> What did the man say was the correct time?
> The boys went swimming in the river.
> The newsboy left the morning paper in the hall.

their
> They left their coats in the hall closet.
> It was their idea to leave early.
> They visit their folks once a month.

them
> We told them to catch the early train home.
> Call them on the phone tonight.
> We invited them for lunch next Thursday.

there
> Go there later in the day.
> They went there without being invited.
> Are there any peaches in the refrigerator?

they
> Will they be over later today?
> They went for a swim in the town pool.
> Are they old enough to vote?

this
> Whose coat is this on the chair?
> I want this box painted yellow.
> Return this book to the library.

31. Three-Word Drill

hard, wood, hardwood

>She is hard to please.
>It was hard work to dig the ditch by hand.
>
>The box was wood inlaid with mother-of-pearl.
>Use a pine wood plank.
>
>This house has hardwood floors throughout.
>Walnut is considered a hardwood.

stage, coach, stagecoach

>Complete the work in easy stages.
>The stage in the theater was unused for many years.
>
>We need a coach for the baseball team.
>Will you coach third base this inning?
>
>My grandfather traveled out west by stagecoach.
>The stagecoach is used as a tourist attraction now.

bare, foot, barefoot

>Her bare arms were tanned from the sun.
>The cupboard was bare.
>
>Who will foot the bill this time?
>The dog sleeps at the foot of the bed.
>
>A barefoot boy with cheeks of tan.
>He went barefoot all summer.

on, ward, onward

>Place the book on the table.
>He left the newspaper on the doorstep.
>
>We live in the fifth ward of the city.
>She will remain in the convalescent ward for a few days.
>
>The army pressed onward in fierce battle.
>The troops were unable to move onward.

pine, apple, pineapple

    The field is beyond the row of scotch pines.
    The robins nested in the pine tree.

    Does an apple a day keep the doctor away?
    My favorite dessert is apple pie.

    Everyone in our family likes fresh pineapple.
    Most pineapples come from Hawaii.

base, ball, baseball

    He was safe at first base.
    The base of the statue was cracking.

    I can throw the ball farther than you.
    We need some new tennis balls.

    He coaches a little league baseball team.
    They went to the baseball game this afternoon.

bath, robe, bathrobe

    I enjoy a warm bath after work.
    The house has two bathrooms.

    Take a robe with you; it's cool outside.
    If you're cold, throw a robe over you.

    I need a new bathrobe.
    I forgot to take my bathrobe on my vacation.

32. Homophonous Words

dime, time, type

    Remember when coffee was a dime a cup?
    I found a dime on the floor.

    Come anytime after three o'clock.
    He had plenty of time to get there.

    Will you type this letter next?
    Use a large size type for this ad.

cold, colt, gold, old

    You will need a coat in this cold weather.
    We sleep in a cold bedroom.

    The colt is in the pasture.
    The Colt revolver was from his grandfather.

    Do you have a gold coin?
    The chain was eighteen karat gold.

    The machine was too old to be repaired.
    He will be sixty years old tomorrow.

bound, mound, mount, pound, pout

    We knew it was bound to happen.
    The book was bound in leather.

    Indian burial mounds were discovered here.
    The builders left a mound of clay in the rear.

    We spent the day at Mount Vernon, Virginia.
    I want to mount these photos in my album.

    We sell our vegetables by the pound.
    That's the last pound of sugar we have.

    Why pout over spilled milk?
    If you don't agree, why pout about it?

coast, ghost, host

    See if the coast is clear.
    They moved to the West Coast years ago.

    You look as though you had seen a ghost.
    He doesn't stand a ghost of a chance to win.

    Mr. and Mrs. Mayfair will be host and hostess at the ball.
    The host was ill on the eve of the party.

feet, feed

    The hallway was six feet wide.
    His feet ached from the long walk home.

    We have to feed the chickens before we go.
    Stop to feed and water the horses.

drain, trade, train, trait

> The kitchen drain is clogged again.
> Drain the tank before you repair it.

> He is an electrician by trade.
> We deal in wholesale trade only.

> They are taking the train this time.
> His train of thought was interrupted by noise.

> John demonstrates the distinguished traits of his dad.
> We wonder who he inherited his bad traits from.

33. Reading *c, z,* and *s*

The *c, z,* and *s* sounds are made with the narrowest opening of the lips, hardly noticeable. The sounds consist of a short exhalation of breath, as in *kiss.*

zero

> Our coldest day was five degrees below zero.
> My license number has four zeros.
> He scored a zero on the test.

zip

> What is your zip code?
> The zipper on my jacket is broken.
> Let's get a little zip into this work.

zone

> We live in a tropical zone.
> The property is zoned for commercial use.
> You gained one hour in each time zone.

sale

> The house has been up for sale for over a year.
> We are having a garage sale this Saturday.
> Olson's is having a sale on women's dresses.

sand

Sand the wood to make it smooth.
The lake has a sand bottom.
We spent the day at the sand dunes.

sauce

Bring home a bottle of chili sauce.
Make a cheese sauce for the broccoli.
What's sauce for the goose is sauce for the gander.

seat

We can seat only eight people at our table.
He tore the seat of his trousers climbing the fence.
The theater will seat three thousand people.

sold

His possessions were sold at auction.
We sold our house in the country.
The house sold for a fair price.

south

We live on the south side of the street.
We go south every winter.
The airport is two miles south of the city.

sun

We watch the sun set on cool evenings.
Almost everybody got sunburned at the beach.
A blazing sun made the city hot and humid.

cent

A 5 percent sales tax was charged.
The morning paper is fifteen cents now.
Gasoline rose to sixty-three cents a gallon this week.

since

I haven't seen him since we left school.
No changes have been made since the war.
The factory has been here since 1950.

send

> Don't forget to send a birthday card to Mary.
> We usually send them by parcel post.
> Send these letters by air mail.

size

> What size shoe do you wear?
> They didn't have my size in hats.
> John needs an extra-large-size sweater.

race

> He lost his last dollar at the horse races.
> They race over a two-mile track.
> His horse is in the fourth race at the fairgrounds.

34. Reading *ch, j, sh,* and Soft *g*

For *ch, j, sh,* and soft *g* as in *germ,* the lips are thrust forward with a narrow opening.

chain

> A heavy chain barred entrance to the road.
> A thin gold chain held her mother's locket.
> His boat was chained to the dock.

cheese

> Give me one pound of swiss cheese, please.
> Let's have ham and cheese sandwiches for lunch.
> Our entire family likes cheesecake.

child

> The youngest child is four years old.
> Each child has his own room.
> He is a very tall child for his age.

chew

> We are not permitted to chew gum in class.
> Who stuck his chewing gum under the chair?
> The steak was tough and hard to chew.

jack

    We always carry two jacks in the car.

    He hit the jackpot on the slot machine.

    You will have to jack the car up an inch.

jingle

    The bells jingle in a slight breeze.

    Coins jingle in my pocket.

    "Jingle Bells" is a favorite Christmas song.

jump

    It's a hop, skip, and jump to the grocery store.

    Do you think you can jump across the stream?

    You jump from rock to rock to get down the mountain.

shadow

    The trees left their shadows on the wall.

    He won without a shadow of a doubt.

    The evening shadows quickly faded.

shape

    The shape and figure I remember; the name I forget.

    The door had an oval shaped window.

    It was an odd shaped vase.

show

    Show Aunt Helen your new dress.

    Let me show you how to do it.

    The town has an art show every fall.

shut

    The plant shut down two assembly lines.

    This is the second shutout he has pitched.

    You forgot to shut the door when you came in.

shoot

    Shoot if you must this old grey head.

    You need a special license to shoot deer.

    They hold an annual turkey shoot in Maine.

general
> The state general assembly adjourned.
> It was a small town with one general store.
> Who is the general of the air force?

gem
> The ring was set with a precious gem.
> The gem was in a museum.
> She is a real gem when you need help.

35. Three-Word Drill

sweet, heart, sweetheart
> Bring home a pound of sweet butter.
> Roses have a sweet smell.

> They have to learn a poem by heart for school.
> Was his heartbeat normal?

> He gave his sweetheart a box of candy.
> Laura is grandfather's little sweetheart.

stir, ring, stirring
> You have to stir the cake batter more than that.
> He won't stir from the TV during football season.

> The ring was too small for her finger.
> They sat in a ring around the campfire.

> The pastor gave a stirring sermon this morning.
> Keep stirring the fudge until it's thick.

hand, bag, handbag
> Please hand me the keys to the house.
> He injured his hand when he fell.

> He used plastic bags for storing food.
> Put the bag of potatoes in a cool place.

> She left her handbag in the car.
> Leather handbags are rather expensive.

drift, wood, driftwood

The snowdrifts were four to five feet high.
Let the boat drift with the current.

The boat was made of teakwood.
We have a good supply of wood for the fireplace.

The beach was full of driftwood from the storm.
He uses the driftwood for wood carving.

price, less, priceless

What is the price of this vase?
We are going out to price a living room set.

He had less than six to choose from.
Train fare is less than plane fare.

The vase was priceless and only on public display.
She gave her priceless jade statue to the museum.

some, body, somebody

Leave some candy for your brother.
Bring home some bacon for breakfast.

She was sunburned over most of her body.
The dress material didn't have any body to it.

Somebody hid the loot in the neighbors' garage.
Somebody will have to be here to answer the phone.

36. Homophonous Words

crew, grew, screw

He had a crew cut when he was young.
They work in crews of three men.

Only the weeds grew in our garden.
The tree grew about five feet in a year.

Use wood screws to hold the board.
We need more screws to finish the job.

shop, job, chop

I hate to shop for groceries.
They have a better selection in the shop across the street.

It's his job to see that the men work daily.
He does odd jobs around people's homes.

The lamb chops are too expensive.
Chop some wood for the fireplace.

bar, mar, par

They will bar the public from the meeting.
Play the first eight bars of the song.

His drinking would mar a perfect evening.
Try not to mar the walls when you clean.

What is the par value of the stock?
His golf score was three below par this morning.

beach, peach

The beach was covered with seaweed.
On hot days everybody is at the beach.

The farmers had a good peach crop this year.
The students earn extra money by picking peaches.

smoke, spoke

Heavy black smoke poured from the chimney.
We cannot smoke during office hours.

The spokes on the wheel were bent.
The principal spoke at the student assembly.

slip, slim

Don't slip on the ice!
The address was on a yellow slip of paper.

He has a slim chance to win.
Mary was always a slim person.

rope, robe, roam

The rope was not long enough.
Tie the rope securely to the post.

The robe is in the hall closet.
You need a warm robe in winter.

My children roam in the forest all summer.
He allows his dog to roam only in his yard.

37. Reading Hard *c*, Hard *g*, *k*, *ng*, *nk*, and *ck*

Hard *c* as in *cat*, hard *g* as in *got*, *k* as in *keep*, *ng* as in *bang*, *nk* as in *bank*, and *ck* as in *crock* are produced by slight movements of the throat just above the Adam's apple that are hardly seen. The lipreader must rely on the context of the sentence to reveal the word used.

can

I can go on Tuesday morning.
See if you can lift this box.
We will need a large can of tomatoes.

cake

I must bake a cake this afternoon.
The mud caked on his shoes.
Take this cake to the church bazaar.

card

Send a postcard when you get to England.
I lost my union card this morning.
Do you have a deck of poker cards?

cook

Let me cook the evening meal.
My brother is the cook in this restaurant.
The island is named after Captain Cook.

crop

We had a good crop of corn this year.
The vegetable crop is ready for picking.
That story crops up every so often.

give

Don't give free advice; it's never used.
We give to charity often.
Can you give me the correct answer?

gold

She wore a white gold ring.
The gold mine operated for fifty years.
Our country is not on the gold standard anymore.

good

He has a very good credit rating.
We saw a very good movie last night.
Walking is good for your health.

get

I think we can get it wholesale.
Let me get you a glass of water.
He failed to get the gist of the story.

keep

My watch keeps good time.
You will have to keep the plant indoors.
We always keep a light burning in the hall.

kick

It's my turn to kick the ball.
He broke his toe when he kicked the door.
See how far you can kick the football.

king

On our vacation we met the king of Norway.
A lion is the king of beasts.
We want a kingsize mattress.

ring

>You can hear the church bell ring.
>She prefers a plain gold wedding ring.
>Did the front doorbell ring?

rank

>Tall, rank grass filled the field.
>He was promoted to the rank of major.
>He is the first person to rise from the ranks.

bank

>The bank is closed on Saturday.
>Our blood bank is in need of donors.
>Borrow the money from the bank.

pick

>We intend to pick apples this afternoon.
>See if you can pick a ripe melon.
>Let him pick the one he thinks is best.

sick

>He will be on sick leave for a month.
>She is sick at heart about the sad news of her brother.
>Two of our family are sick in the hospital.

38. Reading *qu*

Qu takes the sound of *kw*. The *k* is a throat sound, and the *w* is formed by pursing the lips and thrusting them forward.

quaint

>It was a quaint village street.
>She spoke with a quaint southern accent.
>The sentence was quaintly phrased.

quart

>You will need a quart of milk.
>The car needs a quart of oil.
>We can make only two quarts at a time.

queen

Who will be homecoming queen this year?
Queen Elizabeth attended the ball.
I prefer a queen-size bed.

quality

The quality goes in before the name goes on.
Jones's merchandise is of fine quality.
The material was of poor quality.

quarter

The recipe calls for a quarter pound of butter.
Bus fare is now a quarter.
Cut the pie into quarters.

qualify

Would he qualify for the position?
Only one person qualified for the job.
It took years of training to qualify for the work.

question

If you don't understand, ask questions.
His answer was questionable.
I will question his ability to perform the task.

quick

He has a quick temper.
Let's stop for a quick cup of coffee.
His reply was quick and curt.

quiet

I'm looking for a quiet place to read.
He spent a quiet evening at home.
With four children, our home is never quiet.

quilt

We need quilts at the cottage in winter.
My grandmother made this quilt.
The quilt was machine made.

quit

> Ask the children to quit making all that noise.
> Is it time to quit work now?
> We all quit work at the same time.

quote

> Let me quote the figures used.
> He quotes sayings of other people.
> A wrong quote was given for the stock.

quake

> The question made him quake in fear.
> The earthquake caused extensive damage.
> The quake was a shock to the townspeople.

quench

> Give me a drink to quench my thirst.
> Do we have enough water to quench the fire?
> You can quench his ideas with a drop of water.

39. Reading *w* and *wh*

For *w* and *wh* the lips pucker and move forward. The degree of puckering depends on the speed of speech; it is greater in slow speech, much smaller in rapid speech.

wall

> Most people prefer wall-to-wall carpeting.
> The garden was enclosed by a brick wall.
> The livingroom wall was painted light green.

west

> The house is on the west side of the road.
> Go west, young man, go west.
> The western sky was red from the setting sun.

winter

> We had a cold winter last year.
> Her family spends the winters in Florida.
> We didn't have much snow this winter.

wonder

> Can you name the seven wonders of the world?
> I wonder if he will be elected.
> The laboratory is working on a new wonder drug.

wolf

> It is a problem to keep the wolf from the door.
> You can hear the wolf pack howl in the forest.
> He has the reputation of being the office wolf.

woman

> It is often said that "woman's work is never done."
> Will we ever have a woman president?
> Hazel was the only woman at the convention.

white

> Do you think we will have a white Christmas?
> The church will hold a white elephant sale.
> The bride wore a white satin gown.

wool

> In the north you need wool clothing.
> Wool gloves and a wool scarf keep me warm.
> He raises sheep for the wool.

weed

> As usual we now have more weeds than flowers.
> We can weed out the unwanted items later.
> They have to clear the weeds and brush from the land.

wheel

> Our car has a twenty-foot wheel base.
> Somebody stole the front wheel of Tom's bike.
> The wheelbarrow had a wood wheel.

wind

> A warm south wind blew across the plains.
> They got wind of our plans.
> He plays a wind instrument in the band.

work

> They work an eight-hour day at the factory.
> Their work is never done.
> Let him work the problem alone.

walk

> I walk to work every day.
> It's a ten-minute walk from here.
> In case of fire, walk to the nearest exit.

weight

> Do you have a table of weights and measures?
> What is the weight of this box?
> Give me the weight in pounds and ounces.

well

> Ten o'clock and all is well.
> I know him very well.
> Our town has well water.

40. Three-Word Drill

dish, water, dishwater

> Use the small dish for your salad.
> Would you like a dish of ice cream?

> Who will water my plants while I'm on vacation?
> Our well pumps four gallons of water a minute.

> Put more soap in the dishwater.
> The dishwater is not very warm.

fan, fare, fanfare

> He's a baseball fan if there ever was one.
> We use a large fan to circulate the air.
>
> Bus fare is thirty-five cents.
> If you go on Wednesday the fare is ten percent lower.
>
> The parade started with a fanfare of trumpets.
> The new store is opening with a fanfare of advertising.

town, ship, township

> Half the town was flooded in the rainstorm.
> What is the population of our town?
>
> Only a small ship can enter the port.
> The ship is in dry dock for repairs.
>
> A township is usually six miles square.
> They are moving the factory to a township to avoid city taxes.

note, book, notebook

> Make a note of the day we hold our meeting.
> Send a note to my sister to drop by next weekend.
>
> A used-book store might have a copy.
> She has four cookbooks and still can't cook.
>
> Has anyone seen my notebook?
> They have to have a notebook for each subject.

flat, land, flatland

> We own a two-flat building.
> He ran the distance in one minute flat.
>
> The ship is scheduled to land at dawn.
> There is not much vacant land in our city now.
>
> The flatland was good for growing wheat.
> Cattle grazed in the flatland in the valley.

wild, fire, wildfire

Wild horses roamed the plains.
Many wildflowers grow in the desert.

It's nice to sit by a warm fire on a cold night.
Extinguish the campfire when you leave.

The rioting spread like wildfire.
The news spread like wildfire.

41. Homophonous Words

butt, putt, mud, bud, bun, pun

I'll have one slice of ham from the butt end.
He dropped his cigarette butt on the carpet.

John missed his putt by four inches.
I must practice so that I can putt better.

John tracked mud over the floor.
Clean off the mud on your boots.

We have a few buds on the rose bushes.
There are buds on the fruit trees now.

The bakery has hot cross buns today.
Her hair was combed back and tied in a bun.

His sentence turned into a pun accidentally.
Look the word *pun* up in the dictionary.

sign, sight, side, site

Ask him to sign on the bottom line.
Put this "For Sale" sign in the window.

Jerry drives a sightseeing bus downtown.
Never buy anything sight unseen.

Walk on the left side of the street.
You should have sidestepped the question.

This would be a good site for our factory.
He just purchased the site by the railroad.

grade, grain, grate, crate
They have a machine to grade the road.
Use a good grade of bond paper.

The grain will be shipped by boat.
His reply should be taken with a grain of salt.

Clean the fireplace grate.
The noise grates on my nerves.

Set the lobster crates in deep water.
We buy a crate of eggs a month.

mill, pill, bill
The old mill is still running.
He works at the steel mill.

Take one pill four times a day.
He takes four kinds of pills a day.

Our electric bill is due the fifth.
Are all the bills paid?

42. Reading *bl* and *pl*

To form *bl* or *pl*, the lips begin in the natural position for the *b* or *p*; then the tongue touches the palate for the *l*.

blow
He gave a blow by blow description of the fight.
Before you go to bed blow out the candle.
We had a blowout on the way to town.

blank

Fill out this entry blank.

Leave a blank space for your name.

My mind was a total blank.

black

The result of the fight was one black eye.

John is the black sheep of the family.

Be sure to bring home some black shoe polish.

blue

All the children wear blue jeans now.

Paint the bedroom a light blue.

A pair of blue jays have a nest in the tree.

block

Block the wheels so the car can't roll.

His shop is in the next block.

The accident will block traffic for hours.

place

I want to place a bet on the third race.

Win, place, or show I always lose.

Place a knife and fork by each plate.

plate

The plate glass window was broken in the storm.

I'm returning your cake plate.

The coffee urn was silver plated.

plant

We didn't plant the garden until May.

Warm weather enabled the farmers to plant their crops early.

We water the geranium plant once a week.

play

The children usually play at the playground.

I hope the band will play a waltz.

We need someone to play second base.

please

> You can't please everybody.
> Will you please pass the salt?
> Do as you please about the matter.

plot

> The play has an interesting plot.
> We have a small plot of land.
> The town has a plot of this area.

plug

> Father always carried a plug of tobacco.
> The electric plug has a short in it.
> Guess we'll have to plug along on the deal.

plain

> A plain and simple answer was given.
> She lived in the western plains.
> Tom always was a plainspoken person.

bloom

> The cherry blossoms are in full bloom.
> We prefer flowers that bloom all summer.
> Violets bloom in the spring.

blind

> Please close the blind.
> She has been blind since childhood.
> They built a duck blind.

43. Reading *br* and *pr*

For the *b* and *p* in *br* and *pr,* the lips are natural. The *r* is formed by an unseen roll of the tongue.

brain

> It is easy to brainwash some people.
> John is the brain of the firm.
> You really need a brain to figure out that problem.

brand

They will brand the calves next week.
Grants sells only name-brand products.
Marie has her own brand of humor.

break

The dish didn't break when it fell.
He will very likely break the record.
It was a lucky break when he won the lottery.

brick

We prefer a brick house.
John is a bricklayer by profession.
They live in the brick house on the corner.

brown

It is the only brownstone dwelling in town.
May I see a pair of brown sandals, please?
Get the small brown box on the shelf.

brush

Brush your shoes before you go.
I need to brush up on my reading.
That's the fourth brush fire this week.

proceed

We will proceed with the meeting.
The proceeds of the auction were given to charity.
Narrow road ahead — proceed with caution.

prime

Who is the prime minister of England?
Prime beef is expensive these days.
Does anybody here know how to prime a pump?

print

Read the fine print at the bottom.
Please print your name and address.
Have five hundred copies printed.

prompt

> Your prompt reply is requested.
> They give prompt service in this store.
> Return borrowed books promptly.

prepare

> Not many persons are prepared for a rainy day.
> Will someone help me prepare lunch?
> The town wasn't prepared for the heavy snows.

practice

> We should practice what we preach.
> They say practice makes perfect.
> I don't believe he is licensed to practice law.

present

> Ten members were present at the meeting.
> Under present conditions it would not be advisable.
> I can't go at the present moment.

branch

> Our branch office is in Denver.
> Trim the branches on the tree.
> The branches broke under the heavy snow.

price

> I hope he charged the right price.
> The gas stations are having a price war.
> Would the price be cheaper by the dozen?

44. Reading *cl* and *gl*

The *c* and hard *g* in *cl* and *gl* are unseen throat sounds, and the *l* is made with a narrow opening of the lips while the tongue touches the palate. The movement is hardly noticeable, and the lipreader must rely more on the remainder of the word.

claim

He claims she owed him the money for months.
If nobody claims the package you may keep it.
Mary's claim to the property was proved in court.

class

The art class is limited to twenty students.
I'll meet you in the hall after my English class.
The teachers are required to teach six classes a day.

clean

Stella's house is always clean and neat.
The Republicans made a clean sweep in the elections.
Take these clothes to the cleaners.

clear

It took months to get a clear title to the property.
He spoke in a loud, clear voice.
It was a beautiful bowl of clear crystal.

clip

Take these papers and clip them together.
Don wants a money clip for his birthday.
Have the barber clip your hair short on the sides.

cloud

It was a warm, sunny day with no clouds in the sky.
Since her engagement she has been on cloud nine.
The rolling clouds threatened a storm.

club

Our bridge club meets once a month.
I'll have a club sandwich for lunch.
The members voted to build a new club house.

glass

May I have a glass of water, please?
The glass in the window was broken.
Place a water glass by each plate.

glance

> The ball glanced off the roof.
> I will glance over the reports before the meeting.
> Just glance through the book before we leave.

glare

> The sunlight throws a glare on the paper.
> It is rather rude to glare at a person.
> The glaring light has given me a headache.

glad

> The meeting was so lengthy I was glad it was over.
> I will gladly help at the benefit.
> We were glad to learn that Jones was elected mayor.

glove

> John wants a baseball glove for his birthday.
> In this cold weather you need warm gloves.
> I left my gloves at home this morning.

glow

> Winning the race made John glow with pride.
> The room was comfortable from the warm glow of the fireplace.
> Light from the glowworms flickered in the field.

close

> Mary and I have been close friends for years.
> The store closes at nine on Friday.
> Be sure to close the door when leaving.

45. Three-Word Drill

kid, nap, kidnap

> I would like a pair of black kid gloves.
> The kid from the next block delivers our paper.

> Take a short nap before lunch.
> Don't you have a heavier napped rug?

He's not wealthy; why would they kidnap him?
The kidnapper held three persons as hostages.

letter, head, letterhead

Mail this letter to your aunt.
Teach him to write one letter at a time.

How many head of cattle do you have?
Flip a coin; I'll take heads.

Our letterheads are on bond paper.
Don't use the company letterhead for scratch paper.

ward, robe, wardrobe

The fifth ward has the most voters.
The three children are wards of the state.

It's rather cool; we'd better take a robe to the beach.
If you're cold, throw a robe over your shoulders.

Hang your coat in the wardrobe downstairs.
I'm just shopping for a summer wardrobe.

suit, case, suitcase

That color doesn't suit me at all.
Do you have a suit without a vest?

Bring home a case of beer.
His case comes up in court soon.

We had to carry our own suitcases on board.
Get a small and large suitcase to match.

stub, born, stubborn

That's the fourth time he has stubbed his toe this week.
I always carry a pencil stub to jot down notes.

His father was born in France.
The twins were born on different days.

I'm trying to get rid of a stubborn cold.
He's a very stubborn person if there ever was one.

straw, berry, strawberry

That's the last straw.
A straw vote will be taken in October.

Blueberry pie is my favorite.
The berry crop was rather poor this year.

Strawberries need sandy soil.
Grandmother always made strawberry jam.

46. Homophonous Words

deer, dear, tier, tear, near

The deer in the park are tame.
He went to the woods to hunt deer.

Just use "Dear John" when you start the letter.
I think his prices are too dear.

Our seats were in the upper tier.
The book is on the lower tier to the left.

My eyes tear from the smell.
She didn't shed a tear when they parted.

Our home is near the grade school.
Put the chair near the window.

flour, flower

Use whole wheat flour for the bread.
Most flour is bleached these days.

The flower is about ready to bloom.
You will need a larger flower vase.

cart, guard, card

Don't put the cart before the horse.
The cart has not been used for years.

Dogs guard the factory at night.
Armored guards collect the money daily.

Just send a postcard to let them know.
Do you have a deck of cards?

47. Reading *cr* and *gr*

The *c* in *cr* and the *g* in *gr* are throat sounds, and the lip opening is very narrow. For the *r* the lips move forward very slightly and then move to whatever vowel follows.

craft

A small craft is moored in the harbor.
We went to the arts and crafts show.
He is a crafty person.

crash

The airplane made a crash landing in the field.
Three young lads decided to crash the party.
The car skidded and crashed into a light pole.

cream

Bring home a quart of ice cream.
Do you use cream in your coffee?
The cream is in the refrigerator.

credit

His credit balance is in five figures.
Many people buy everything on credit.
I misplaced my credit card for the store.

crop

He has a thick crop of hair.
This rain will really help the farmers' crops.
That old tale crops up every so often.

crisp

 The morning was crisp with cool air.
 We were served a crisp lettuce salad.
 The crisp air foretold the coming of winter.

crystal

 My watch crystal broke this morning.
 No two snow crystals are alike.
 The flowers were placed in a crystal vase.

grand

 We had a grand time on our vacation.
 Ed won five grand in the lottery.
 Our grand piano needs tuning.

great

 That house was owned by my great grandfather.
 He raises great danes as a hobby.
 Everybody had a great time at the party.

green

 Green beans and green peppers grew in the garden.
 Too often the green-eyed monster rears its head.
 Paint the walls a pale green.

grind

 Have the butcher grind the round steak.
 I can remember when we had to grind our own coffee.
 The old mill still grinds corn and wheat.

ground

 The ground was soggy from two weeks' rain.
 On what grounds did she get her divorce?
 The building stands on leased ground.

group

 Put them in groups of three.
 A group of Girl Scouts attended the meeting.
 A large group of parents attended the PTA meeting.

grow

The tree will grow two feet a year.
Will this plant grow in this climate?
We grow our own vegetables in the back lot.

grape

The valley is famous for its grapes.
Grapevines covered the fence around the house.
Oranges and grapefruit are expensive this year.

48. Reading *dr* and *tr*

For the *d* and *t* in *dr* and *tr,* the tongue touches the palate; for the *r* the tongue rolls downward. This movement is hardly seen; any noticeable movement will be a very narrow opening of the lips followed by whatever vowel is used next.

draft

I have prepared a rough draft of my speech.
Send a bank draft for payment.
The open window caused a draft in the room.

drain

The drain in the kitchen is plugged again.
His sickness was a drain on our savings.
This drainpipe drains only rainwater.

drift

Snowdrifts five feet high blocked the highway.
The beach was filled with driftwood.
I don't think I got the drift of the story.

draw

The pump is too small to draw enough water.
Mr. Jones is at his lawyer's to draw up a will.
With these expenses we will have to draw money from the bank.

drill

In that area they have to drill their own wells.
Mike runs a drill press at the factory.
Drill a half-inch hole in the board.

drive

The drive shaft on the pump needs oiling.
On rainy days we drive to work.
The club will have a membership drive.

drum

William is the drum major in the Legion band.
At our house we need chickens with four drumsticks.
Our school drum and bugle corps won the state contest.

trade

That company has been in the building trade for years.
The company's trade name is well known.
He owns the Trade Wind Motel down the road.

traffic

Turn right at the next traffic light.
The traffic is heavy on weekends only.
I don't like to drive my car when traffic is heavy.

train

His train of thought was interrupted by the phone.
The train is over three hours late.
The team's training camp is in Florida.

trip

We intend to take a trip south this winter.
She sprained her ankle when she tripped.
This is our fifth trip to Europe.

true

The arrow flew straight and true to the target.
Who would know the true value of the painting?
I believe he gave a true description of the accident.

trunk

> The tree trunk was eighteen inches thick.
> Grandmother's trunk of old clothes is in the attic.
> Somebody stole the spare tire from the trunk of the car.

try

> Please try to be on time for the meeting.
> I would like to try on a pair of shoes.
> The tryouts for football are on Friday.

trust

> The property was placed in trust for the children.
> A check was drawn on the First Trust & Savings Bank.
> It is foolish to place trust in a person you just met.

49. Three- and Four-Word Drill

pan, cake, pancake

> You will need a larger pan than that.
> I don't like to wash the pots and pans.
>
> We prefer chocolate cake at our house.
> She had a five-tier wedding cake.
>
> Use the ready-mix pancake flour.
> The scouts are having a pancake breakfast Saturday.

pen, man, ship, penmanship

> They use ballpoint pens at school.
> We should have made the pig pens larger.
>
> I think that man worked here last year.
> Hire another man for the shipping department.
>
> The ship left port an hour ago
> See that they ship this order today.
>
> The schools should teach penmanship.
> Today penmanship seems to be a lost art.

pep, per, mint, peppermint

I don't have enough pep to work any longer.
The coach is giving the team a pep talk.

These are a dollar per dozen.
The cost is on a per annum rate.

Our company mints coins for foreign countries.
Garnish the salad with mint leaves.

I never tasted peppermint ice cream.
The children like peppermint candy.

road, side, roadside

Are we on the right road?
The road is badly in need of repairs.

Place it on the left side of the door.
They live on the north side of town.

You are not permitted to park on the roadside.
They operate a roadside restaurant.

for, bid, forbid

Do we have to dress for dinner?
He served as senator for two terms.

Our bid for the contract was too high.
He overbid his last hand and was set.

We forbid the children to play in the street.
Why he was forbidden entrance was unknown.

sales, man, salesman

Our monthly sales are up 10 percent.
Most of our sales are in the evening.

We need another man on our team.
The man waited three hours for an interview.

Jones is the best salesman we have.
He's a door-to-door book salesman.

50. Homophonous Words

type, time, dime

> Type a copy of this report for our records.
> Use a typewriter with small type.
>
> It's about time we left for home.
> What time is it?
>
> He saved silver dimes for years.
> When I started working, bus fare was only a dime.

grim, grip, crimp, crib

> He led a grim life on the farm.
> Some people have a grim outlook of the future.
>
> His grip was stolen at the station.
> Get a good grip on the box before you lift it.
>
> The wire was too crimped to be used.
> The high cost put a crimp in my vacation plans.
>
> The water crib is a mile from shore.
> We will need more corn cribs as the stock increases.

sign, side, sight

> Sign on the dotted line.
> Put up a "For Sale" sign on the property.
>
> It's on the left side of the house.
> Choose sides for a ball game.
>
> Not a taxi was in sight during the storm.
> The sight of the flag was inspiring.

51. Reading *fl* and *fr*

To form the *f* sound in *fl* or *fr*, the upper teeth touch the inside of the lower lip. For the *l* the tongue touches the palate. The *r* is a roll of the tongue.

flag
> They will erect a flagpole in the park.
> We display the flag on national holidays.
> I hope we can flag a taxi.

flat
> Her answer was a flat refusal.
> They live in the two-flat across the street.
> Charge a flat rate for each mile.

flash
> A flash of lightning filled the sky.
> The heavy rains caused a flash flood in the valley.
> Take the flashlight with you.

flip
> Will someone flip the light switch in the hall?
> Why don't we flip a coin to see who goes?
> Press the button and the cover flips up.

flood
> They are putting floodlights in the ball park.
> The low land floods every time it rains.
> We received a flood of letters protesting the issue.

flow
> The river flows to the south.
> Not much water flows over the dam now.
> You can't make water flow uphill.

fly
> When do the robins fly south?
> Our intent is to fly to Europe.
> Jones hit a pop fly to left field.

frame

> Our window frames need painting.
> The framework for the building has been completed.
> The picture was in a gold frame.

free

> You are allowed three hundred dollars' worth of imports
>   duty free.
> They left of their own free will.
> We traveled the freeway to Ohio.

front

> I'll meet you in front of the post office.
> The front of our house faces west.
> Enter at the front of the bus.

fruit

> We will have fruit salad for dessert.
> The trees are too young to bear fruit.
> Order a fruitcake for the holidays.

fry

> I'd like an order of french fries please.
> Every Friday night the restaurant has a fish fry.
> Use olive oil to fry the chicken.

frank

> He gave a frank and honest answer.
> Please enclose a franked envelope.
> A frank reply would embarrass some people.

fresh

> Trout and bass are fresh-water fish.
> Do not touch fresh paint.
> Get a loaf of fresh bread and some fresh vegetables.

floor

> Is this the second or third floor?
> The house has oak floors throughout.
> The club has a new floor show every other week.

52. Three-Word Drill

water, proof, waterproof

> The flooding river has reached its high water mark.
> Our town has very good well water.

> He has no proof who actually stole the money.
> Have someone proofread this document.

> It was supposed to be a waterproof coat.
> Use a waterproof paint on the outer wall.

whole, sale, wholesale

> It was not a whole set of dishes.
> The whole family was invited to the dinner.

> The vacant lot is not for sale.
> Our sales usually run for seven days.

> All merchandise is in wholesale lots.
> The wholesale price was 15 percent less.

tea, pot, teapot

> We seldom drink tea at our house.
> Would you like a glass of iced tea?

> Use a small pot to boil the water.
> I hate to clean the dirty pots and pans.

> You forgot to clean the teapot this morning.
> We need a larger teapot.

some, body, somebody

> John left some books for you to read.
> He left some samples of wood to be used.

> The lifeguards found the body on the beach.
> The car body was dented on the left side.

> Did somebody ring the doorbell?
> Will somebody help me lift this board?

type, write, typewrite

Do you know what type blood you have?
Use a large type for the heading.

Just write a short note to thank them for the gift.
Write your name and address on this card.

I have to typewrite a letter for Mr. Thomas.
She can typewrite one hundred words a minute.

care, less, careless

At present I am under the care of Dr. Smith.
He is in intensive care at the hospital.

I have less money in the bank than I thought.
Use less milk in your coffee.

She is very careless with her money.
That was a rather careless remark to make.

wonder, land, wonderland

I wonder why the children are late coming home.
We wonder if he will accept the position.

The land is very good for farming.
Half the land is under water every spring.

The area is a wonderland for winter sports.
The valley was a wonderland of flowers.

53. Homophonous Words

bail, mail, pail, bale, male, pale

Post a bail bond of twenty-five dollars.
He was held without bail.

Our mail delivery is late today.
Mark this mail to be posted on the thirteenth

Put the pail in the garage.
This pail holds three gallons of water

The horses eat a bale of hay a day.
Don't bale all the hay; stack some in the field.

They chose a male puppy.
His male pride was hurt.

She looks rather pale today.
I think pale blue would look nicer.

said, scent, send, set, cent, sent

Who said the answer was correct?
What she said to him nobody knows.

The dogs quickly picked up the scent of the fox.
The perfume has a pleasant scent.

Don't send his order until the end of the month.
The company will send Mr. Jones to Europe.

We have a new television set.
For the time being, set the books on the floor.

Our state has a sales tax of five cents on the dollar.
This one cent piece was minted the year I was born.

I sent him to the store over an hour ago.
Where was the package sent?

bill, mill, pill

This bill was paid three months ago.
All our mail seems to be bills these days.

Due to the drought the mill had to stop.
My great grandfather built the mill.

The pills for my sinus were quite expensive.
Take one pill four times a day.

hand, hat, had

His left hand is empty.
Will you hand me the salt, please?

I wear a hat only during the winter.
Put your hat in the hall closet.

They had to leave on the early train.
We had a hard time finding his house.

harm, harp, arm

She claims she would not harm a hair on his head.
Be careful not to harm the puppy.

They will harp on that subject for months.
My sister played the harp in the orchestra.

Please don't sit on the arm of the sofa.
She was greeted with open arms.

54. Reading *sl, sm,* and *sp*

For the *s* in *sl, sm,* and *sp,* there is a very quick, narrow opening of the lips followed by a roll of the tongue to the palate for the *l* or the lips natural position for the *m* or *p*.

slack

There is too much slack in the rope.
October is the slack time at our factory.
The children need slacks for school.

slam

I had to slam on the brakes to avoid an accident.
Please don't slam the door when you leave.
Did you have to slam the book on the table?

slow

Our clock was ten minutes slow.
We walked at a slow pace through the park.
You'd better slow down a little; there is a speed trap ahead.

slip

I usually fill out the deposit slip at the bank.
Be careful; don't slip and fall on the ice.
Why don't we slip out the back door?

slice

    Don't slice the ham too thick.

    Give me a slice of beef that is well done.

    Would you like a slice of rye bread?

small

    She has two small children to care for.

    I need a small box for some odds and ends.

    Just give me a small piece of cake.

smell

    The dog has a keen sense of smell.

    You can smell the fumes from the factory on warm days.

    We keep a bottle of smelling salts in the cabinet.

smoke

    Grandfather smoked a pipe for years.

    You are not allowed to smoke on the train.

    They need hickory wood to smoke the hams.

smooth

    We need a smooth surface to work on.

    The board is smooth on one side only.

    Most politicians are smooth talkers.

smile

    It is better to smile than to frown.

    I could not help but smile at his answer.

    She greets all persons with a friendly smile.

space

    We have a space heater in the garage.

    They need more space for storage.

    You have to pay for a parking space at the station.

speak

    Do you speak a foreign language?

    He had to speak in a loud voice to be heard.

    Mr. Jones would like to speak to you before you leave.

speed

The speed limit is 55 m.p.h.
Mary got a ticket for speeding last night.
We are going to the speedboat races today.

spin

Most spiders spin their webs at night.
Grandma still spins her own yarn for knitting.
The motor spins at a high rate of speed.

sport

Be a good sport and loan me ten bucks.
My favorite sport is football.
I'm thinking of getting a sport coat this fall.

55. Reading *sn, st,* and *sw*

For the *sn* and *st* the opening of the lips is narrow, a hiss for the *s* sound, with the tongue touching the teeth for the *n* and *t* sounds. The *sw* is made with a very narrow opening for the *s*; then the lips pucker and extend forward slightly for the *w*.

snake

Some people dread snakes.
John has a snake for a pet.
We live in rattlesnake country.

snap

That cold snap lasted a week.
It was a snap decision that was wrong.
The door has a snap lock.

snow

A heavy snowfall is predicted for tomorrow.
It was ideal snow for skiing.
You can see the snow-capped mountains.

sneak

He tried to sneak out without doing his homework.
Do you think we can sneak out without Mom knowing?
Some sneak thief stole the purses from the wardrobe room.

stack

We have two haystacks in each field.
Stack the newspapers in a neat pile.
I had a stack of pancakes for breakfast.

stair

Don't leave your books on the stairs.
On warm nights we sit on the back stairs.
A narrow stairway led to the attic.

stalk

Chop up a crisp stalk of celery.
Remember the story "Jack and the Beanstalk"?
Cornstalks and pumpkins decorated the hall.

stamp

Do you have a postage stamp?
The dish was stamped sterling silver.
Stamp this bill "paid" and return it.

state

Hawaii was the last state admitted.
The building was in a poor state of repair.
We have to file a state income tax.

sweep

A new broom sweeps clean.
He won first prize in the sweepstakes.
We have to sweep the factory every night.

swell

Her arm began to swell from the bee sting.
The ocean swells made the passengers seasick.
The swelling was reduced by hot applications.

swim

> It is wise to learn to swim.
> He would swim two miles a day.
> The water was too cold for swimming.

swing

> Do you think we can swing this deal on our terms?
> In grandma's day porch swings were common.
> Everybody's at the swing concert in the park.

56. Three-Word Drill

port, hole, porthole

> Our cabin is on the port side of the ship.
> Why not serve a port wine with dinner?
>
> The street is full of chuckholes since the rain.
> His cigarette burned a hole in the carpet.
>
> You don't get much air through this porthole.
> The porthole was under water during the rough seas.

life, boat, lifeboat

> There's not much life in this town after ten o'clock.
> Throw him a life preserver.
>
> We had to beach the boat during the storm.
> He just looks at a boat and gets seasick.
>
> The lifeboat patrols the harbor all summer.
> A lifeboat check will be made before we leave port.

in, tend, intend

> Don't stand out in the rain.
> You'll find the keys in the drawer.
>
> It's my night to tend the furnace.
> More people should tend to their own affairs.

We intend to go to the concert this week.
He intends to get a degree in law.

mail, box, mailbox

Any mail for me today?
Be sure to mail this letter today.

Get a box to store these books.
Every now and then he brings me a box of candy.

The mailbox must have your name on it.
The mailbox is on the corner.

master, mind, mastermind

He is scoutmaster for the church troop.
He's a jack of all trades, master of none.

He has a mind of his own.
More people should mind their own business.

Mr. Jones masterminded the project.
You have to be a mastermind to read his writing.

tea, room, tearoom

We usually have tea for supper.
We drink only Chinese tea.

There is not much room in the hall closet.
The room was filled with flowers.

The tearoom does a brisk business.
Two sisters own the tearoom.

57. Homophonous Words

beech, peach, beach

The beech tree was planted too near the house.
I'd like a pack of Beechnut gum, please.

We had homemade peach pie for dessert.
The farmers expect a good crop of peaches.

On holidays the beach is crowded.
It's too cold to be at the beach today.

mark, park, bark

Put a question mark after the sentence.
Have John mark the route on the map.

The state park closes October first.
There was no place to park the car.

The birch tree has white bark.
The dog barks at anyone near the house.

day, pay, may

On what day did we pay the phone bill?
Only one more day before my vacation.

He was willing to pay ten percent interest.
Use the pay phone in the station.

The month of May has thirty-one days.
The bill was due on the first of May.

knock, lock, dock

Knock on the door to see if anybody's home.
There's a knock in the motor.

Get a new lock for the front door.
Be sure to lock the doors when you leave.

The ocean liner was too big to use the dock.
The loading dock is in the rear of the building.

red, rend, read, rent, wren

His car was white with red trim.
The home had red cedar closets.

Three policemen had to rend the loot from the robber.
I'm afraid lightning will rend the tree.

We read the book years ago.
Has he read the fine print on the form?

How much is the rent for the apartment?
Get a "For Rent" sign at the store.

The wren house must be cleaned each year.
We think the same wren comes every year.

view, few
We have a fine view of the mountain.
Is the property within view of the lake?

Only a few people attended the meeting.
Try to put through a few more orders today.

58. Reading *thr, shr,* and *str*

For *thr,* the lips touch the upper teeth and the tongue curves up and moves backward—a movement hard to see. For *shr,* the lips narrow and project slightly forward and the tongue curves up and moves backward—also hard to see. For *str,* the *s* is formed by a very narrow opening of the lips, the *t* by the tongue touching the palate, and the *r* by a roll of the tongue, followed by the vowel.

thread
Bring home a spool of black thread.
Will you thread this needle for me?
We need a heavy thread to mend the tent.

three
Only three persons were present at the meeting.
Our address is three-four-three Stout Street.
I have to leave at three to catch my train.

thrive
The plants must have sun to thrive.
He has a thriving business in town.
Not many people could thrive on his diet.

throw

    Throw the ball to first base.

    Who can throw this ball the farthest?

    Try to throw with your left hand.

through

    Thank heavens, I'm through for the day.

    His office is through that door.

    He succeeded through hard work.

shrink

    Wool will shrink in hot water.

    That material will shrink when you wash it.

    The material is guaranteed not to shrink.

shrub

    We have to plant these shrubs today.

    The florist didn't have a large selection of shrubs.

    Our shrubs need pruning this spring.

strand

    She wore a strand of pearls.

    A ship was stranded on the beach.

    I gave mother a strand of beads for Christmas.

string

    Tie a string around your finger.

    The children will string beads in class today.

    We have string beans for supper.

stream

    They sang "Down by the Old Mill Stream."

    This is one of the best trout streams in the state.

    A steady stream of water flowed from the pump.

stretch

    It's time for the seventh inning stretch.

    He is famous for stretching the truth.

    How far will the rubber band stretch?

strike

> The men at the factory went on strike at noon.
> Wait till the clock strikes the hour.
> The army will strike at dawn.

strong

> A strong wind blew from the west.
> We need a strong piece of rope.
> The army marched ten thousand strong.

stroke

> She had a mild stroke last week.
> A stroke of lightning hit the tree.
> He swam breaststroke on the swimming team.

59. Three-Word Drill

free, way, freeway

> It seems I don't have any free time anymore.
> The supermart gives a free dish with each ten-dollar purchase.

> There must be an easier way to remove paint.
> Tom will show you the way to go home.

> The freeway is always crowded on Sunday nights.
> It took the state three years to build a freeway.

finger, print, fingerprint

> I burned my finger on the hot pot.
> It seems that everyone has a finger in the pie.

> Always read the fine print at the bottom.
> Have them print the invitations today.

> The police took his fingerprints.
> He left his fingerprints on the wallpaper.

quick, sand, quicksand

He is noted for his quick thinking.
A quick decision is not always advisable.

You have to sand the wood with the grain.
They play for hours in the sandbox.

The left shore is nothing but quicksand.
The lowlands contain quicksand and muck.

meat, ball, meatball

Only the best grade of meat is handled at his shop.
They get their meat directly from the wholesale house.

Throw the ball to third base.
That's the second golf ball I've lost today.

May I have another meatball, please?
I think I'll have the spaghetti with meatballs.

hall, way, hallway

Pay your taxes at the village hall.
Just walk down the hall and turn left.

You do it your way; I'll do it my way.
Their house is a short way from here.

The hallway is rather narrow.
That office is at the end of the hallway.

bill, board, billboard

Pay the bills by the fifth of the month.
This is the fifth bill we have sent.

He left without paying his board bill.
We need a board two inches thick.

The billboard must be two hundred feet from the highway.
What is the rental for the billboard?

60. Homophonous Words

kind, kite, guide, height

>What kind of paper will you need?
>He was noted for his kind deeds.
>
>We made our own kites when we were young.
>What did Benjamin Franklin prove when he flew his kite?
>
>Let me guide you through the forest.
>A guide will explain the exhibits.
>
>You will have to increase the height of the house.
>What is the height of the Washington Monument?

thick, thing, think

>Use a thick plank to cover the hole.
>The walls were twelve inches thick.
>
>We don't have a thing in the house for lunch.
>I could not think of a thing to say.
>
>Think of a good excuse not to go.
>I don't think that is the right answer.

lamb, lap, lamp

>Let him lead the lamb home.
>We'll have lamb stew for supper.
>
>He's living in the lap of luxury.
>Eighty laps of the pool is one mile.
>
>Leave the hall lamp lit when you leave.
>We need another lamp in this room.

61. Reading *spl* and *spr*

For the *s* in *spl* and *spr,* the lips form a very narrow opening and extend slightly, then close for the *p*. For the *l* the tongue touches the palate, and for the *r* it rolls upward and back, unseen.

splash

    He fell into the pool with a big splash.

    The Joneses are having a splash party in their pool.

    Everybody was splashed with water from the broken pipe.

splendid

    It was a splendid display of fireworks.

    That was a splendid idea.

    We had a splendid time at the party.

split

    I split my ballot when I voted.

    Our home was a split-level with six rooms.

    I have a splitting headache this evening.

splurge

    We splurged and bought new shoes.

    We're saving money to splurge on our vacation.

    Because of our doctor bills, we can't splurge on clothes.

spray

    The bridesmaid carried a spray of roses.

    We used a spray gun to paint the house.

    Spray the plants with a fine spray of water.

spread

    Spread the peanut butter evenly.

    I bought new bedspreads for our room.

    The cornfields spread for miles along the road.

spring

    After the long winter, spring will be welcome.

    The weeds seem to spring up overnight.

    Cool, clear water came from the spring.

sprinkle
>We have to sprinkle the lawn today.
>Be sure to sprinkle the coconut on the cake.
>We just had a light sprinkle of rain here.

spruce
>I want to spruce up a little before dinner.
>Blue spruce trees were planted on the farm.
>The valley was covered with spruce trees.

spry
>I'm not as spry as I used to be.
>Grandfather is just as spry as ever.
>We need a young, spry person to run the machine.

sprout
>The beans are beginning to sprout in the garden.
>Brussels sprouts are my favorite vegetable.
>Many Chinese dishes contain bean sprouts.

62. Consonant and Vowel Drill: *b, p, m*

short *a, b,*
>bă ba ba ba - ba ba ba ba
>ba ba ba ba - ba ba ba ba
>bat bat bat - bat bat bat
>bat bat bat - bat bat bat
>bat the ball - bat the ball
>bat the ball - bat the ball

short *a, p*
>pă pa pa pa - pa pa pa pa
>pa pa pa pa - pa pa pa pa
>pat pat pat - pat pat pat
>pat pat pat - pat pat pat
>pat on the back - pat on the back
>pat on the back - pat on the back

long *a, m*

mā ma ma ma - ma ma ma ma
ma ma ma ma - ma ma ma ma
male male male - male male male
male male male - male male male
male watchdog - male watchdog
male watchdog - male watchdog

short *e, b*

bĕ be be be - be be be be
be be be be - be be be be
bell bell bell - bell bell bell
bell bell bell - bell bell bell
bell just rang - bell just rang
bell just rang - bell just rang

long *e, m*

mē me me me - me me me me
me me me me - me me me me
meter meter meter - meter meter meter
meter meter meter - meter meter meter
meter for gas - meter for gas
meter for gas - meter for gas

long *i, b*

bī bi bi bi - bi bi bi bi
bi bi bi bi - bi bi bi bi
bide bide bide - bide bide bide
bide bide bide - bide bide bide
bide your time - bide your time
bide your time - bide your time

long *o, b*

bō bo bo bo - bo bo bo bo
bo bo bo bo - bo bo bo bo
bolt bolt bolt - bolt bolt bolt
bolt bolt bolt - bolt bolt bolt
bolt of cloth - bolt of cloth
bolt of cloth - bolt of cloth

short *u, b*

bŭ bu bu bu - bu bu bu bu
bu bu bu bu - bu bu bu bu
bump bump bump - bump bump bump
bump bump bump - bump bump bump
bump on the head - bump on the head
bump on the head - bump on the head

63. Consonant and Vowel Drill: *d, n, t*

short *a, d*

dă da da da - da da da da
da da da da - da da da da
dab dab dab - dab dab dab
dab dab dab - dab dab dab
dab of butter - dab of butter
dab of butter - dab of butter

long *a, n*

nā na na na - na na na na
na na na na - na na na na
name name name - name name name
name name name - name name name
name of your dog - name of your dog
name of your dog - name of your dog

short *e, t*

tĕ te te te - te te te te
te te te te - te te te te
test test test - test test test
test test test - test test test
test the battery - test the battery
test the battery - test the battery

long _e, d_

    dē de de de - de de de de
    de de de de - de de de de
    deed deed deed - deed deed deed
    deed deed deed - deed deed deed
    deed to the property - deed to the property
    deed to the property - deed to the property

short _i, t_

    tĭ ti ti ti - ti ti ti ti
    ti ti ti ti - ti ti ti ti
    tint tint tint - tint tint tint
    tint tint tint - tint tint tint
    tint it light tan - tint it light tan
    tint it light tan - tint it light tan

long _i, n_

    nī ni ni ni - ni ni ni ni
    ni ni ni ni - ni ni ni ni
    nine nine nine - nine nine nine
    nine nine nine - nine nine nine
    nine flowers in bloom - nine flowers in bloom
    nine flowers in bloom - nine flowers in bloom

short _o, n_

    nŏ no no no - no no no no
    no no no no - no no no no
    not not not - not not not
    not not not - not not not
    not at home - not at home
    not at home - not at home

short _u, d_

    dŭ du du du - du du du du
    du du du du - du du du du
    dump dump dump - dump dump dump
    dump dump dump - dump dump dump
    dump the dirt here - dump the dirt here
    dump the dirt here - dump the dirt here

long *u*, *t*

tū tu tu tu - tu tu tu tu
tu tu tu tu - tu tu tu tu
tune tune tune - tune tune tune
tune tune tune - tune tune tune
tune the piano - tune the piano
tune the piano - tune the piano

64. Consonant and Vowel Drill: *f* and *v*

short *a*, *f*

fă fa fa fa - fa fa fa fa
fa fa fa fa - fa fa fa fa
fast fast fast - fast fast fast
fast fast fast - fast fast fast
fast train service - fast train service
fast train service - fast train service

long *a*, *v*

vā va va va - va va va va
va va va va - va va va va
vase vase vase - vase vase vase
vase vase vase - vase vase vase
vase on the table - vase on the table
vase on the table - vase on the table

short *e*, *f*

fĕ fe fe fe - fe fe fe fe
fe fe fe fe - fe fe fe fe
fed fed fed - fed fed fed
fed fed fed - fed fed fed
fed the dog - fed the dog
fed the dog - fed the dog

long *e*, *v*

 vē ve vc ve - ve ve ve ve
 ve ve ve ve - ve ve ve ve
 vcto veto veto - veto veto veto
 veto veto veto - veto veto veto
 veto the bill - veto the bill
 veto the bill - veto the bill

short *i*, *f*

 fĭ fi fi fi - fi fi fi fi
 fi fi fi fi - fi fi fi fi
 fish fish fish - fish fish fish
 fish fish fish - fish fish fish
 fish in the brook - fish in the brook
 fish in the brook - fish in the brook

long *i*, *v*

 vī vi vi vi - vi vi vi vi
 vi vi vi vi - vi vi vi vi
 vine vine vine - vine vine vine
 vinc vine vine - vine vine vine
 vine of tomatoes - vine of tomatoes
 vine of tomatoes - vine of tomatoes

long *o*, *f*

 fō fo fo fo - fo fo fo fo
 fo fo fo fo - fo fo fo fo
 fold fold fold - fold fold fold
 fold fold fold - fold fold fold
 fold the paper - fold the paper
 fold the paper - fold the paper

short *u*, *v*

 vŭ vu vu vu - vu vu vu vu
 vu vu vu vu - vu vu vu vu
 vulgar vulgar vulgar - vulgar vulgar vulgar
 vulgar vulgar vulgar - vulgar vulgar vulgar
 vulgar language - vulgar language
 vulgar language - vulgar language

long *u*, *f*

    fū fu fu fu - fu fu fu fu
    fu fu fu fu - fu fu fu fu
    fuse fuse fuse - fuse fuse fuse
    fuse fuse fuse - fuse fuse fuse
    fuse blew out - fuse blew out
    fuse blew out - fuse blew out

65. Consonant and Vowel Drill: *j* and *ch*

short *a*, *ch*

    chă cha cha cha - cha cha cha cha
    cha cha cha cha - cha cha cha cha
    champ champ champ - champ champ champ
    champ champ champ - champ champ champ
    champ in swimming - champ in swimming
    champ in swimming - champ in swimming

long *a*, *j*

    jā ja ja ja - ja ja ja ja
    ja ja ja ja - ja ja ja ja
    jade jade jade - jade jade jade
    jade jade jade - jade jade jade
    jade and diamond ring - jade and diamond ring
    jade and diamond ring - jade and diamond ring

short *e*, *j*

    jĕ je je je - je je je je
    je je je je - je je je je
    jelly jelly jelly - jelly jelly jelly
    jelly jelly jelly - jelly jelly jelly
    jelly sandwich for lunch - jelly sandwich for lunch
    jelly sandwich for lunch - jelly sandwich for lunch

long _e, ch_

    chē che che che - che che che che
    che che che che - che che che che
    cheese cheese cheese - cheese cheese cheese
    cheese cheese cheese - cheese cheese cheese
    cheese and tomato - cheese and tomato
    cheese and tomato - cheese and tomato

short _i, ch_

    chĭ chi chi chi - chi chi chi chi
    chi chi chi chi - chi chi chi chi
    chip chip chip - chip chip chip
    chip chip chip - chip chip chip
    chip off the old block - chip off the old block
    chip off the old block - chip off the old block

long _i, ch_

    chī chi chi chi - chi chi chi chi
    chi chi chi chi - chi chi chi chi
    chime chime chime - chime chime chime
    chime chime chime - chime chime chime
    chime of the bells - chime of the bells
    chime of the bells - chime of the bells

long _o, j_

    jō jo jo jo - jo jo jo jo
    jo jo jo jo - jo jo jo jo
    joke joke joke - joke joke joke
    joke joke joke - joke joke joke
    joke is on me - joke is on me
    joke is on me - joke is on me

short _u, j_

    jŭ ju ju ju - ju ju ju ju
    ju ju ju ju - ju ju ju ju
    jump jump jump - jump jump jump
    jump jump jump - jump jump jump
    jump with joy - jump with joy
    jump with joy - jump with joy

66. Consonant and Vowel Drill: *l*

short *a, l*

    lă la la la - la la la la
    la la la la - la la la la
    land land land - land land land
    land land land - land land land
    land for farming - land for farming
    land for farming - land for farming

long *a, l*

    lā la la la - la la la la
    la la la la - la la la la
    lake lake lake - lake lake lake
    lake lake lake - lake lake lake
    lake in the woods - lake in the woods
    lake in the woods - lake in the woods

short *e, l*

    lĕ le le le - le le le le
    le le le le - le le le le
    left left left - left left left
    left left left - left left left
    left turn only - left turn only
    left turn only - left turn only

long *e, l*

    lē le le le - le le le le
    le le le le - le le le le
    lead lead lead - lead lead lead
    lead lead lead - lead lead lead
    lead the parade - lead the parade
    lead the parade - lead the parade

short *i, l*

lĭ li li li - li li li li
li li li li - li li li li
lift lift lift - lift lift lift
lift lift lift - lift lift lift
lift this box - lift this box
lift this box - lift this box

long *i, l*

lī li li li - li li li li
li li li li - li li li li
life life life - life life life
life life life - life life life
life of the party - life of the party
life of the party - life of the party

long *o, l*

lō lo lo lo - lo lo lo lo
lo lo lo lo - lo lo lo lo
lone lone lone - lone lone lone
lone lone lone - lone lone lone
lone person at home - lone person at home
lone person at home - lone person at home

short *u, l*

lŭ lu lu lu - lu lu lu lu
lu lu lu lu - lu lu lu lu
lump lump lump - lump lump lump
lump lump lump - lump lump lump
lump of clay - lump of clay
lump of clay - lump of clay

67. Consonant and Vowel Drill: *r*

short *a, r*

    ră ra ra ra - ra ra ra ra

    ra ra ra ra - ra ra ra ra

    rank rank rank - rank rank rank

    rank rank rank - rank rank rank

    rank and file - rank and file

    rank and file - rank and file

long *a, r*

    rā ra ra ra - ra ra ra ra

    ra ra ra ra - ra ra ra ra

    race race race - race race race

    race race race - race race race

    race to the train - race to the train

    race to the train - race to the train

short *e, r*

    rĕ re re re - re re re re

    re re re re - re re re re

    rent rent rent - rent rent rent

    rent rent rent - rent rent rent

    rent an apartment - rent an apartment

    rent an apartment - rent an apartment

long *e, r*

    rē re re re - re re re re

    re re re re - re re re re

    recount recount recount - recount recount recount

    recount recount recount - recount recount recount

    recount the money - recount the money

    recount the money - recount the money

short *i, r*

    ri ri ri ri - ri ri ri ri
    ri ri ri ri - ri ri ri ri
    ring ring ring - ring ring ring
    ring ring ring - ring ring ring
    ring on her finger - ring on her finger
    ring on her finger - ring on her finger

long *i, r*

    ri ri ri ri - ri ri ri ri
    ri ri ri ri - ri ri ri ri
    right right right - right right right
    right right right - right right right
    right on time - right on time
    right on time - right on time

long *o, r*

    ro ro ro ro - ro ro ro ro
    ro ro ro ro - ro ro ro ro
    roll roll roll - roll roll roll
    roll roll roll - roll roll roll
    roll call today - roll call today
    roll call today - roll call today

short *u, r*

    ru ru ru ru - ru ru ru ru
    ru ru ru ru - ru ru ru ru
    run run run - run run run
    run run run - run run run
    run away now - run away now
    run away now - run away now

68. Consonant and Vowel Drill: *s* and *z*

short *a, s*
      să sa sa sa - sa sa sa sa
      sa sa sa sa - sa sa sa sa
      sack sack sack - sack sack sack
      sack sack sack - sack sack sack
      sack of potatoes - sack of potatoes
      sack of potatoes - sack of potatoes

long *a, s*
      sā sa sa sa - sa sa sa sa
      sa sa sa sa - sa sa sa sa
      safe safe safe - safe safe safe
      safe safe safe - safe safe safe
      safe at first base - safe at first base
      safe at first base - safe at first base

short *e, s*
      sĕ se se se - se se se se
      se se se se - se se se se
      send send send - send send send
      send send send - send send send
      send a post card - send a post card
      send a post card - send a post card

long *e, z*
      zē ze ze ze - ze ze ze ze
      ze ze ze ze - ze ze ze ze
      zero zero zero - zero zero zero
      zero zero zero - zero zero zero
      zero weather again - zero weather again
      zero weather again - zero weather again

short *i*, *z*

     zĭ zi zi zi - zi zi zi zi
    zi zi zi zi - zi zi zi zi
    zip zip zip - zip zip zip
    zip zip zip - zip zip zip
    zip code your mail - zip code your mail
    zip code your mail - zip code your mail

long *i*, *s*

    sī si si si - si si si si
    si si si si - si si si si
    sign sign sign - sign sign sign
    sign sign sign - sign sign sign
    sign your name - sign your name
    sign your name - sign your name

long *o*, *s*

    sō so so so - so so so so
    so so so so - so so so so
    sole sole sole - sole sole sole
    sole sole sole - sole sole sole
    sole of my shoe - sole of my shoe
    sole of my shoe - sole of my shoe

69. Consonant and Vowel Drill: *w* and *wh*

long *a*, *wh*

    whā wha wha wha - wha wha wha wha
    wha wha wha wha - wha wha wha wha
    whale whale whale - whale whale whale
    whale whale whale - whale whale whale
    whale of a story - whale of a story
    whale of a story - whale of a story

short *e, wh*

whĕ whe whe whe - whe whe whe whe
whe whe whe whe - whe whe whe whe
when when when - when when when
when when when - when when when
when shall we go? - when shall we go?
when shall we go? - when shall we go?

long *e, w*

wē we we we - we we we we
we we we we - we we we we
weeds weeds weeds - weeds weeds weeds
weeds weeds weeds - weeds weeds weeds
weeds in the lawn - weeds in the lawn
weeds in the lawn - weeds in the lawn

short *i, wh*

whĭ whi whi whi - whi whi whi whi
whi whi whi whi - whi whi whi whi
which which which - which which which
which which which - which which which
which one is larger? - which one is larger?
which one is larger? - which one is larger?

long *o, wh*

whō who who who - who who who who
who who who who - who who who who
whole whole whole - whole whole whole
whole whole whole - whole whole whole
whole wheat bread - whole wheat bread
whole wheat bread - whole wheat bread

70. Three-Word Drill

frame, work, framework

Most homes in this town are frame buildings.
The picture frame was made of plastic.

Some people don't know what a hard day's work is.
Work on the bridge started this week.

The framework on the tower is finished.
In a building that size the framework has to be steel.

stop, light, stoplight

We want to stop at the fruit stand on the way home.
Shall we stop in the next town for lunch?

That's the fourth light bulb that has burned out today.
It's the light blue dress in the window.

The stoplight favors east-and-west traffic.
Turn left at the next stoplight.

wrist, watch, wristwatch

He broke his wrist playing football.
This is the fourth week his wrist has been in a cast.

He prefers to watch the ballgame on TV.
Pocket watches are coming back in style.

He gave her a wristwatch for her birthday.
My wristwatch is at the jeweler's being repaired.

high, way, highway

The top shelf is too high for me to reach.
I think the price of the sofa is too high.

Most people choose the easy way out.
Peter is working his way through college.

The highway is closed for repairs.
You can travel fifty-five miles an hour on the highway.

trade, mark, trademark

He's going to trade his car in.
The building trade is slack this year.

Put a red mark on the trees you want removed.
Place a checkmark on the items you need.

The package does not have a trademark on it.
They want to design a new trademark.

ring, worm, ringworm

Did the doorbell ring just now?
You can hear the church bells ring.

We need some worms for fishing.
The apples were all wormy.

She has a bad case of ringworm on her arm.
The doctor is treating the ringworm with a sulfa drug.

71. Homophonous Words

mound, mount, pound, bound

Level the mounds of dirt in back of the house.
They think the mounds are prehistoric.

Mount the horse from its left side.
That is Mount McKinley over there.

Give me one pound of butter, please.
It is only sold in one-pound packages.

The book was bound in leather.
He's bound to get hurt playing in that old building.

tried, dried

She tried on four or five pairs of shoes.
I tried but could not lift the stone.

They dried their clothes in the sun.
You can use dried prunes for coffee cake.

hand, hat, had

    He has a very large hand.
    The shop features handmade clothing.

    A gust of wind blew his hat off.
    I left my hat on the car seat.

    We had to change a tire on the way over.
    They finally had the broken window replaced.

few, view

    Only a few people attended the meeting.
    Put a few flowers in this vase.

    The new building blocks our view of the lake.
    A post blocked our view of the football field.

beak, meek, peek, peak

    The bird's beak was dark brown.
    Most birds of prey have a curved beak.

    She is a meek person.
    The meek shall inherit the earth.

    Take a peek to see if the baby is all right.
    Care to peek at our new home?

    He has reached the peak of his career.
    Mount McKinley is the highest peak in North America.

bull, pull

    The bull topped eleven hundred pounds.
    The bull pen is empty.

    My dentist will pull my tooth tonight.
    Pull the rope through the window.

72. Reading Suffixes

A suffix is an affix occurring at the end of a word. Examples of suffixes are -ed, -ful, -ing, -ive, -ly, -ment, -ness, -tion, and -ure.

Study this chapter while watching yourself in a mirror. You can learn a lot about lip formation simply by forming each letter as explained. First, watch the movement of your tongue and lips as you speak each letter slowly. Then increase the speed of the word until it is spoken at a normal rate, noting how the lip movement changes from a slow, exaggerated formation to the formation of the naturally spoken word.

Let's take each suffix individually and look at the speech formation of several words with suffixes attached.

form, formed
f: upper teeth to lower lip;
o: lips opened wide and thrust forward;
r: (unseen) roll of tongue;
m: lips close naturally.
For the suffix -ed, the formation is a medium extended opening of
    the lips, with the tongue to the palate for the d.

fist, fistful
f: upper teeth to lower lip;
i: corners of lips natural, opening narrow;
st: s is a slight hiss and the tongue touches behind the upper teeth for
    the t.
In the suffix -ful, the f is formed with the upper teeth to the lower lip;
    the short u with a medium opening, lips thrust slightly forward,
    and the l with the tongue behind the upper teeth.

bat, batting
b: lips natural;
a: lips wide open with a slight extension at the corners;
t: tongue just behind the upper teeth.
The suffix -ing is formed by a narrow opening of the lips, slightly
    extended.

pass, passive

p: lips natural;

a: lips wide open;

s: lips close to make a narrow opening for the *s* hiss.

For the suffix *-ive,* the *i* is made with a narrow opening; for the *v* the upper teeth touch the lower lip, which makes a slight, quick in-and-out movement.

lone, lonely

l: tongue just behind the upper teeth;

o: lips pucker with a wide opening and become more puckered;

n: tongue to palate (the *e* makes no sound).

For the suffix *-ly,* the tongue touches just behind the upper teeth, then the lips form a narrow extended opening.

fulfill, fulfillment

f: upper teeth to lower lip;

u: opening medium, lips slightly puckered and thrust forward;

l: tongue just behind upper teeth;

f: teeth to lower lip;

i: narrow opening with corners of lips remaining natural;

l: tongue just behind upper teeth.

For the suffix *-ment,* the *m* is formed with the lips closed; the *e* is made by a medium opening with the lips slightly extended at the corners; the *nt* is formed with the tongue near the upper teeth.

loose, looseness

l: tongue behind upper teeth;

oo: lips pucker and extend forward and opening is narrow while corners pucker;

s: unseen hiss; the *e* is silent.

In the suffix *-ness,* *n* is made with the tongue behind the upper teeth, *e* with a medium opening and the corners of the lips extended; *ss* is an unseen hiss.

elect, election

e: medium opening, lips slightly extended;

l: tongue behind upper teeth;

e: medium opening, lips slightly extended;

ct: spoken as one sound, tongue touching behind upper teeth.

The suffix *-tion* is pronounced *shun.* For *sh,* lips pucker, opening narrow; the *un* is a quick drawing back of the lips with the tongue touching behind the upper teeth.

73. Reading Unseen Words

As you are learning to lipread, you will sometimes find it hard to lipread each and every word in a sentence. Even if you are experienced you will note that not every word spoken is lipreadable. You must train yourself to fill in the words you missed.

First, as suggested before, you must know what the topic of conversation is. Let's take the following situation.

One of your fellow employees comes in about twenty-five minutes late. Upon entering, he speaks the following sentence:

"The train was thirty minutes late this morning."

The situation will let you know what the sentence was about. Of this conversation you only lipread the following words:

". . . . train . . . . thirty . . . . late. . . . ."

From the words that you actually lipread it is not a problem to fill in the missing words: "The train was thirty minutes late this morning."

For practice, read the following situations and the identifiable words in the sentence spoken. See if you can fill in the missing words. The words do not have to be exact; all you need is a general understanding of the conversation. Given the situation, see if you can grasp what is spoken. The complete sentences are at the end of the chapter.

1. You ask your neighbor about her sons John and Bill. She replies: ". . . . . fishing . . . . . lake. . . . ."

2. Your husband asks for an electric light bulb and you ask why he needs one. His reply: ". . . light . . . . . hall . . . . . . burned. . . . ."

3. You ask Carl's mother if Carl is home. Her reply: "Carl and Mary . . . . . . Burger King . . . lunch. . . . ."

4. An insurance salesman inquires about a friend of yours, handing you a card. He says: ". . . . . his . . . . . . address . . . . . card. . . . . ."

5. You take the keys to the car and start to leave the house. Your husband says: ". . . . . put . . . . gas . . . . . car . . . . oil. . . . . ."

6. The people across the street are away on vacation. There is a police car in front of the house and policemen are walking around the property. Your neighbor next door comes over and says: ". . burglar . . . . house . . . . . . the street last. . . . ."

7. You are seated in the kitchen. Your wife comes in the door carrying a bag of groceries, sets them on the table, and says: ". . . . . . . two . . . . bags . . groceries . . . . . car, ... bring . . . . in?"

8. You invited your brother and his wife for Sunday lunch. They arrive a half hour late. Upon entering, he says: ". . . . . late . . . . . . flat tire . . . . . way. . . . ."

9. You are seated in the living room with your wife. A storm is brewing outside. Suddenly, with a clap of thunder, a heavy rain starts falling. Your wife gets up from the chair and says to you: ". . . windows . . . . . bedrooms upstairs . . . open . . . . . . close. . . . ."

10. The weather has been very warm for the last few days. Your husband looks at the outdoor thermometer and says: ". . . temperature . . . dropped . . . . degrees, ... turn . . . . . . conditioner off. . . ."

11. You are preparing the figures for your income tax when the neighbor drops in. He asks what you are doing, and you explain you are getting the necessary figures together to fill out your income tax. He then asks: ". . . . . . going . . fill . . . . . . form . . . . have . . . IRS do . . . . . you?

Many sounds in spoken words have no seen lip movements. Even if a word in a sentence is fully lipreadable you may miss it. This chapter is written to train you to think quickly and fill in the missing words while you lipread the rest of the sentence.

If you have filled in the blank spaces in the practice sentences, it will be of considerable help in your efforts to lipread. The full sentences as spoken are as follows:

1. John and Bill have gone fishing at the lake today.
2. The light in the hall lamp is burned out.
3. Carl and Mary went to Burger King for lunch today.
4. Write his name and address on this card for me.
5. When you're out put some gas in the car and have the oil checked.
6. A burglar broke into the house across the street last night.
7. There are two more bags of groceries in the car; will you bring them in?
8. Sorry we're late; we had a flat tire on the way here.
9. The windows in the bedrooms upstairs are open; help me close them.
10. The temperature has dropped to seventy-five degrees; we can turn the air conditioner off now.
11. Are you going to fill out the form yourself or will you have the IRS do it for you?

74. Three-Word Drill

ever, green, evergreen

It seems we won't ever get there.
Who would ever think he solved the crime?

How about some fresh green beans for supper?
Paint the rear bedroom a light green.

Grandmother planted the evergreen trees.
The robins built a nest in the evergreen tree.

grape, fruit, grapefruit

How much are grapes a pound today?
We prefer seedless grapes.

Usually some fresh fruit is on the menu daily.
She served a fruit salad for dessert.

Get pink grapefruit next time.
The back of the car was loaded with grapefruit and oranges.

finger, nail, fingernail

He hit his finger with the hammer.
The thief left no fingerprints.

Use a larger nail to hold the board.
Get some nails and a hammer from the garage.

Some people have long fingernails.
Clean your fingernails before you go to school.

crow, bar, crowbar

That crow has been around for years.
She finally found something to crow about.

The bar opens at five o'clock.
He was barred from the meeting.

We'll need a crowbar to pry the boards loose.
My crowbar is rusty from disuse.

down, grade, downgrade

Write down what he says at the meeting.
We have down pillows on our bed.

Jane enters third grade next year.
A poor grade of paper was used.

The road is downgrade all the way into town.
Business has been on the downgrade for some time.

75. Homophonous Words

wide, wind, wine, whine, white

> The room is fifteen feet wide and eighteen feet long.
> The road is forty feet wide through town.

> I forgot to wind my watch this morning.
> Wind the yarn in a ball.

> Serve port wine with the dinner.
> If they move into an apartment, there goes his wine cellar.

> You can hear the tires whine on the pavement.
> She's the type that always finds something to whine about.

> Use a sheet of plain white paper.
> Wear your white blouse today.

down, town, doubt

> They don't have enough down payment to buy the home.
> I prefer a down pillow.

> The town was named after his grandfather.
> The next town is twenty-three miles away.

> I doubt he will be elected this time.
> We doubt his team will win.

charm, sharp

> She wore a gold charm bracelet.
> The coin is his good luck charm.

> Be careful; there is a sharp curve ahead.
> This knife is not very sharp.

76. Reading Common Sentences

In our usual day-to-day conversations with people, the same three- or four-word sentences are used over and over. In the following short sentences, study the lip movement word for word until you can grasp the sentence in its entirety.

Sentence	Phonetic pronunciation with seen lip movement
Brush your teeth.	br<u>ŭsh</u> yŏŏr tēth
Answer the phone.	ănsər thə fō<u>n</u>
She just left.	sh<u>ē</u> j<u>ŭst</u> lĕ<u>ft</u>
Any mail today?	ĕn<u>ĭ</u> mā<u>l</u> təd<u>ā</u>
Write it down.	r<u>ī</u>t <u>ĭt</u> d<u>oun</u>
Water the plants.	w<u>ôt</u>ər thə pl<u>ănts</u>
Close the door.	klō<u>z</u> thə d<u>ō</u>r
Mail this letter.	m<u>āl</u> thĭ<u>s</u> lĕtər
Hold the phone.	hō<u>l</u>d thə fō<u>n</u>
How's the weather today?	h<u>ouz</u> thə wĕthər təda
I don't want any.	<u>ī</u> d<u>ō</u>nt wŏnt ĕn<u>ĭ</u>
Pass the salt.	p<u>ăs</u> thə s<u>ô</u>lt
Sit over here.	s<u>ĭt</u> ō<u>v</u>ər hĭr
What time is it?	hwŏ<u>t</u> t<u>ī</u>m <u>ĭ</u>z <u>ĭt</u>
Close the window.	klō<u>z</u> thə w<u>ĭ</u>ndō

Here are some additional common sentences.
When are we going?
Open the door.
Come over early.
Supper will be ready soon.
Turn on the TV.
Mow the lawn.
Shovel the snow.
Are you tired?
Get some gas.

Pay this bill.
How much do I owe you?
Take the bus.
Do you have a match?
How are you?
Wash the dishes.
Take a bath.
Drive the car.
Come with me.
Did you hear the news?
Turn off the TV.
Open the door.

77. Three-Word Drill

class, mate, classmate

Nothing but high-class merchandise is sold here.
The botany class is planning a field trip.

I cannot find the mate of this shoe.
He is first mate on the vessel.

We were classmates in college.
I lost my list of classmates from high school.

foot, ball, football

Our house is at the foot of the hill.
One foot is larger than the other.

Why doesn't he pitch a fast ball?
My golf ball landed on the green.

It's football season again.
His knee was injured in the football game.

light, house, lighthouse
The bright light makes my eyes water.
We had a light rain this morning.

That house has been vacant for over a year.
Our house was sold in less than a week.

The lighthouse has been in use since 1856.
No one wants the job as lighthouse keeper.

safe, guard, safeguard
The safe was too heavy to move.
No one knows the combination to the safe anymore.

It's my turn for guard duty tonight.
They have guards stationed at all doors.

An iron railing will be installed as a safeguard.
Trained dogs are used as a safeguard for the plant.

tar, get, target
All they did was put some tar where the roof leaked.
The driveway is tar and gravel.

Try to get the children to come for supper.
We only get the evening paper.

He missed the target by a mile.
The police have target practice once a month.

water, proof, waterproof
Add one gallon of water.
We have well water in our town.

Do they have any proof that he did it?
This is 100 proof bonded whisky.

The raincoat is guaranteed to be waterproof.
Tar the boards to make them waterproof.

78. Homophonous Words

to, too, two, do, due, dew, new, knew

> We usually walk to the store.
> Let us drink to your health.
>
> It is too far to walk.
> There are too many of us in this small room.
>
> We have a two-car garage.
> It's a two-story building.
>
> He didn't do his homework last night.
> I have to do the laundry today.
>
> The note is past due.
> Your note will be due one year from today.
>
> The morning dew covered the lawn.
> The air was damp from the heavy dew.
>
> We want to purchase a new car.
> I need some new clothes.
>
> He knew he was not correct.
> They knew it was an old building.

charm, sharp

> She wore a gold charm bracelet.
> Laura is a very charming person.
>
> Be careful; the knife is very sharp.
> The road takes a sharp turn to the left at the corner.

trip, trim, drip

> Our trip out west was wonderful.
> Don't trip on the broken step.
>
> Keep in trim by going to the gym.
> The house has oak trim throughout.
>
> We need a can of drip coffee.
> Fix the drip in the faucet.

old, cold, gold, hold

How old is my aunt?
The boy is seven years old.

It is cold this morning.
I have a severe cold today.

My gold watch was stolen.
The coin has one ounce of gold.

Please hold the door open for me.
Hold the other end of the board.

grime, crime, gripe

Soap and water remove most grime.
In industrial plants, grime is common.

Crime is on the increase in our city.
It's a crime to have to work so hard.

He gripes about the work every day.
Mary constantly gripes about her health.

79. Reading Words Ending in -*age*

age

Are your children of voting age?
He graduated from school at an early age.

cage

She was only a bird in a gilded cage.
Put the canary in the cage.

page

Someone tore page 63 out of this book.
What page was that news item on?

rage

She flew into a rage that lasted an hour.
Wide lapels are the rage this winter.

wage

> The metal shop pays a $1.95 hourly wage.
> What is the minimum wage?

damage

> Children, please do not damage the furniture.
> Considerable damage was caused by the heavy rains.

forage

> The natives of Australia had to forage for food.
> His cattle forage for their own food.

garage

> They decided to build a two-car garage.
> Their garage is attached to the house.

passage

> They booked passage on a tramp steamer.
> Passage of the oil bill by Congress is expected.

manage

> Mr. Jones will manage the grocery department.
> In spite of her age she can manage her affairs quite well.

sage

> Name the seven sages of old Greece.
> You can use sage to flavor the roast.

rummage

> The church will hold its rummage sale this Saturday.
> I'll have to rummage through these boxes one of these days.

savage

> Kind words will soothe the savage beast.
> The dog was so savage it was constantly chained.

storage

> There is not much room for storage in the closet.
> The firm needs storage space for the new shipment of goods.

bandage

> The doctor had to bandage the cut.
> Don't wrap the bandage too tight.

sewage

The county will build a new sewage plant this year.
If the new subdivision is built the sewerage system will be needed.

village

Our village does not have a fire department.
All streets in the village are paved.

luggage

You are allowed only two pieces of luggage on the plane.
Our luggage was lost on the trip.

80. Three-Word Drill

back, fire, backfire

Bring the book back in a week.
Back the car carefully.

Start a fire in the fireplace.
The village is getting a new fire truck.

The car engine backfires now and then.
The gun is so rusty it might backfire if you use it.

every, day, everyday

The clock chimes every hour on the hour.
He speaks so loudly you can hear every word.

Let's go shopping some day next week.
It rained for two days and nights.

These are my everyday clothes.
Rain seems to be an everyday occurrence.

time, table, timetable.

Call me any time after six in the evening.
He spends his leisure time fishing.

The coffee table has a glass top.
Set the table for two more people.

The new train timetable is wrong.
Will there be a timetable change for daylight saving time?

steeple, chase, steeplechase

The church steeple needs to be painted.
Did the heavy winds damage the church steeple?

Our dog is too lazy to chase a rabbit.
It would be foolish to chase the robber.

Where is the nearest steeplechase course?
One race daily is a steeplechase.

farm, yard, farmyard

Most farms around here are dairy farms.
We still farm twelve acres for our own use.

Dress material is often a yard wide.
The lawn in the backyard needs to be mowed.

Chickens ran loose in the farmyard.
Our farmyard fence needs to be painted.

lamp, post, lamppost

The lamp is too low for reading.
We keep an oil lamp for emergencies.

Will you post this letter for me?
Send a postcard when you get to California.

He carved his initials on the lamppost.
All wooden lampposts will be replaced with metal ones.

walk, out, walkout

The walk to the store is good exercise.
It's a five-minute walk to the train station.

He was out at first by a mile.
We live a mile out of town.

That's the third walkout at the plant.
Carl lost a month's pay due to the walkout.

81. Homophonous Words

cheer, sheer, jeer, shear
>Try to cheer him up a little.
>I'm hoarse from cheering for our team.
>
>It will be sheer folly even to try.
>The sheer curtains were too short.
>
>The audience jeered the speaker unmercifully.
>Did you come to the meeting to jeer or cheer?
>
>They will shear the sheep in early spring.
>The shears are too dull to cut anything.

be, pea, me, bee, meek, beak, peak, peek
>To be or not to be is the question.
>It is wonderful to be in love.
>
>The restaurant has pea soup once a week.
>Let's have peas for a vegetable tonight.
>
>Leave me out of that kind of deal.
>She tried to blame me for her error.
>
>The quilting bee meets on Thursday in the church.
>He was stung by a bumblebee.
>
>The meek shall inherit the earth.
>She is too meek to speak up.
>
>The bird has a curved beak.
>The eagle tore the flesh with its beak and talons.
>
>The mountain peak is snow-capped all year.
>He has just about reached the peak of his career.
>
>Take a peek to see if the cake is done.
>Peek in the window to see if they are home.

pay, bay, may

Let me pay the bill this time.
She forgot to pay the water bill.

Their home is on Cape Cod Bay.
The dogs held the burglar at bay.

The fruit trees bloom in May.
Bill may change jobs this summer.

bass, pass, mass

He sings bass in the choir.
The bass are biting today.

I have a season's pass for the pool.
Let me pass the papers.

The church has a mass at six o'clock in the morning.
A cold mass of air came from the north.

see, sea

Somehow I can't see his point of view.
See who rang the doorbell.

She collects rare sea shells.
For a change the sea is calm.

82. Reading Numbers

In our daily routines we constantly use numbers and figures — house numbers, phone numbers, prices, the amount of change to be given or received, bank statements, license numbers, and numerous other items. A lipreader must constantly be on the alert to see that he properly understands the figures spoken. The reason for this is that the following numbers are homophonous:

eight, nine	sixteen, sixty
thirteen, thirty	seventeen, seventy
fourteen, forty	eighteen, eighty
fifteen, fifty	nineteen, ninety

If you requested a phone number from a person and the reply was: "Area code six hundred — one thirteen — fifteen fifty," it is easy to see that the homophonous numbers *thirteen, fifteen,* and *fifty* could be easily misunderstood. When this situation occurs, politely request that the numbers be written down, or ask, "Did you say the number was six hundred — one, one, three — one, five, five, zero?"

In stores and supermarkets it is easy to grasp the figures given. For example, Pot roast is ninety-eight cents today. Toothpaste is eighty-three cents for the seven-ounce tube. Pork and beans are twenty-one cents a can. Watermelon is seven cents a pound.

In large department stores where clothing, furniture, refrigerators, rugs, and other higher-priced items are sold, it is best to check the price given. Request the salesperson to repeat the price; further, as most merchandise in these categories bears a price tag, you can look at the tag to see if you really understood the price.

From your own experiences you can anticipate the probable price of an item: under one dollar, one dollar to ten dollars, ten dollars and up. Then the answer will be somewhat expected and you can lipread the reply more easily.

83. Reading Names and Places

Personal names and place names are used rather infrequently, and it can be hard for a lipreader to grasp the name or place quickly.

Paul and Mary will move to New Mexico this fall.
John will do a year of postgraduate work in New York.
Jean's mother and father have a small farm in Iowa.
The Thompsons moved to Minneapolis, Minnesota.
The plane Charles is taking goes to Los Angeles and makes a
  stop at Las Vegas, Nevada.
Barbara and Bob moved here from Florida three years ago.
My children will take a trip to Washington, D.C., next sum-
  mer.
Our neighbors' relatives came from Montreal, Quebec, for a
  short visit last week.

Their vacation trip took them through Wisconsin, Minnesota, South Dakota, and Iowa.

They always take their vacation in winter and go to Miami, Florida.

Frank and Eileen ski in northern Michigan.

Theresa and John still have a home in Springfield, Illinois.

Carl always gets a basket of grapefruit from Texas.

When James retired he and Evelyn moved to South Carolina.

Tom and Jane have lived in Chicago all their lives.

Eleanor and I would like to see the Kentucky Derby just for the fun of it.

They want to travel through the Gulf Coast States, Florida, Alabama, Mississippi, and Louisiana, in the early spring.

Our plane is nonstop from Chicago to Atlanta, Georgia.

Rose's father still works in the steel mill in Pennsylvania.

Oscar, Frank, Bill, and Sidney are forming a car pool to and from the station.

84. Reading Long Sentences

When you are learning to lipread, a sentence of eight to ten words is ideal. If a sentence becomes lengthy, it has a tendency to become somewhat complicated and the lipreader becomes "lost" in the middle of it. If you lose the chain of words, make an effort to grasp the essence of the remainder of the sentence; then your mind can quickly flash back and fill in the portion you missed. Let's take a sentence to see how the chain of thought builds up in a longer sentence.

We are going.

We are going to the supermart.

We are going to the supermart for some groceries and meat.

We are going/ to the supermart/ for some groceries and meat/ early this afternoon.

With practice, lengthy sentences will become fairly easy to follow. For more practice try the following sentences:

We went to the museum.
We went to the museum last week.
We went to the museum last week to see the exhibits.
We went to the museum last week to see the exhibits from Egypt.
We went to the museum/ last week/ to see the exhibits/ from Egypt/ of King Tut.

That old frame house.
That old frame house down the street.
That old frame house down the street burned to the ground.
That old frame house down the street burned to the ground last night.
That old frame house/ down the street/ burned to the ground/ last night/ when no one was at home.

I have to move my plants.
I have to move my plants to the neighbors' garage.
I have to move my plants to the neighbors' garage this afternoon.
I have to move my plants to the neighbors' garage this afternoon, as they promised to water them.
I have to move my plants/ to the neighbors' garage/ this afternoon/ as they promised to water them/ while we are on our vacation.

The chairman of the board of our company.
The chairman of the board of our company will deliver his speech.
The chairman of the board of our company will deliver his speech at the annual meeting.
The chairman of the board of our company will deliver his speech at the annual meeting of the stockholders.
The chairman of the board of our company/ will deliver his speech/ at the annual meeting/ of the stockholders/ this morning.

The children surprised me last week.
The children surprised me last week with their own idea of reading a book.

The children surprised me last week with their own idea of reading a book every Tuesday evening.

The children surprised me last week/ with their own idea of reading a book/ every Tuesday evening/ instead of watching TV.

Henry will retire in a few years.

Henry will retire in a few years and is thinking of buying a home in Florida.

Henry will retire in a few years and is thinking of buying a home in Florida to spend the winter months.

Henry will retire in a few years/ and is thinking of buying a home in Florida/ to spend the winter months/ in a warmer climate.

We went to see Carl and Mabel.

We went to see Carl and Mabel on the West Coast.

We went to see Carl and Mabel on the West Coast this summer.

We went to see Carl and Mabel on the West Coast this summer, never realizing what a long, hard drive it would be.

We went to see Carl and Mabel/ on the West Coast this summer/ never realizing what a long, hard drive it would be/ over the mountains.

85. Three-Word Drill

gate, way, gateway

Close the gate when you leave.
Who left the gate open last night?

We must find a way to economize.
In a polite way, just refuse his offer.

Use the rear gateway when leaving.
A locked gateway kept people out.

shoe, lace, shoelace

He will need a larger size shoe than this.
Do you have this style shoe in brown?

Old lace curtains covered the windows.
I don't care for the lace trim on the dress.

My shoelace broke on the way home.
Tie a double knot in your shoelace.

any, one, anyone

We don't have any butter.
Tell the milkman not to leave any milk today.

One at a time, please.
He will be home in one hour.

Anyone for tennis today?
Anyone over twenty-one can vote.

out, board, outboard

The wind blew the candle out.
He was out of work for three months.

I need a new cover for my ironing board.
A two-foot board will be long enough.

His boat has two outboard motors.
The outboard motor was ten horsepower.

counter, sign, countersign

There was a long line at the checkout counter.
Don't leave your purse on the store counter.

Have the lawyer sign these papers.
All street signs are on the north side of the street.

He was unable to get anyone to countersign his loan.
Have the bank countersign the deed.

screw, driver, screwdriver

Use a one-inch flathead screw.
Better use brass screws so they won't rust.

Who is the driver of this car?
Sam wants to be a truck driver when he grows up.

Pry the lid open with this screwdriver.
The screwdriver is in the tool kit.

sand, paper, sandpaper

Our lake has a sand bottom.
The liner struck a sandbar at low tide.

Bring home the evening paper.
We need ruled paper for school.

Prepare the wood with fine sandpaper.
Use sandpaper on the rusted spots before you paint.

86. Homophonous Words

bubble mumble

Perhaps a bubblebath will relieve the tension.
Most children chew bubblegum.

Somehow he seemed to mumble through his speech.
He mumbles his words when he dictates.

juice, choose, shoes

We usually have some fruit juice for breakfast.
You can buy canned grapefruit juice.

Let mother choose the color.
Let her choose a gift.

Her purse, shoes, and gloves were the same color.
I can't seem to find the right size shoes.

awl, all, haul, hall

He needs an awl to punch holes in his belt.
Most shoemakers have awls; why not try there?

All are present and accounted for.
Mail all the postcards today.

That company won't haul heavy machinery.
Rent a trailer and haul it yourself.

The music hall was built in 1910.
The machine shop used to be a dance hall.

pump, bump, mumps
The village pump isn't working.
We had to pump the story out of her.

Don't bump the car ahead of us.
He bruised his shin when he bumped into the chair.

All my children have had the mumps.
There is an epidemic of mumps in town.

cause, gauze
All she does is cause trouble with the neighbors.
Who caused the accident?

I think I'll get gauze curtains for the bedroom.
Get some gauze bandages from the drugstore.

refuse, review
You can hardly refuse an offer like that.
Does anyone know why she refused his proposal?

The troop passed in review.
He wants a full review of the firm's assets.

thought, thawed
At the time I thought his answer was correct.
He's deep in thought about his business.

The ice thawed quickly in the warm weather.
Frozen food that has thawed should not be refrozen.

87. Reading Seen and Unseen Letters

In normal speech the consonants that are throat and tongue sounds have no lip movement. When the speaker has a well-formed lip movement the consonants formed by tongue movement (*th, l, t, d,* etc.) can be seen. Some speakers have a tendency to use less lip movement than others.

In normal speech, a person speaks vowels more loudly, or at a greater volume, than consonants. When a person speaks in a low-volume voice, the lip movement is lessened and the throat and tongue movements are less visible than in normal speech. As you progress in lipreading, even though a word has letters unseen in lip movements, you will be able to lipread that word by inserting the missing unseen lip movements. You do this by learning and constantly practicing the word and by knowing how the word fits into the sentence. As mentioned earlier, a general knowledge of the topic of conversation is of considerable help.

The following sentences show the seen and unseen lip movement of words in complete sentences. In general, the phonetic pronunciation is given. All letters seen as a lip movement are underscored.

1. Show me the way to go home.
   shō̲ mē̲ thə wā̲ tōō̲ gō̲ hō̲m.

2. It takes me five minutes to walk to the train.
   ĭt tāks̲ mē̲ fī̲v mĭnŭts̲ tōō̲ wôk̲ tōō̲ thə trān̲.

3. They are taking a time and motion study at the plant today.
   thā̲ är tāk̲ĭng ə tĭm̲ ănd mo̲shən (shŭn) stŭ̲dē̲ ăt thə plănt̲ tədā̲.

4. We have to go to the lawyer's office this evening to sign some legal papers.
   wē̲ hăv̲ tōō̲ gō̲ tōō̲ thə lôyərz̲ ôfĭs̲ thĭs̲ ēvnĭng tōō̲ sīn̲ sŭm̲ lēgəl pāpərz̲.

5. Last night's storm did a lot of damage in our town.
   lăst nīts̲ stō̲rm dĭd ə lŏt ŭv̲ dămĭj ĭn our̲ toun̲.

6. Request all members of the club to be present at the next meeting.
   rĭkwĕst ôl mĕmbərz ŭv thə klŭb tōō bē prĕzənt ăt thə nĕkst mētĭng.

7. My cousin and his wife are coming for lunch next Sunday.
   mī kŭzən ănd hĭz wīf är kŭmĭng fôr lŭnch nĕkst sŭndī.

8. We are planning to go to the coast, as Joe gets four weeks' vacation this year.
   wē är plănĭng tōō gō tōō thə kōst ăz Jō gĕts fôr wēks vākāshən thĭs yĭr.

9. Pay these bills by check; they are due on the tenth of the month.
   pā thēz bĭlz bī chĕk thā är dū ŏn thə tĕnth ŭv thə mŭnth.

10. To avoid the crowds we do most of our shopping early in the morning.
    tōō əvoid thə kroudz wē dōō mōst ŭv our shŏpĭng ûrlĭ ĭn thə môrnĭng.

In the following sentences the sounds with unseen lip movement have been omitted.

11. Now is the time for all good men to come to the aid of their country.
    -ow ĭz --ə -īm fô- ô- -ŏŏ- mĕ- -ōō -ŭm -ōō --ē ā- ŭv --ĕ- -ŭ---ĭ.

12. Since the new speed limit went into effect it takes us three days to drive to Florida.
    sĭ-s --ə -ū spē- -ĭmĭ- wĕ-- ĭ--ōō ĭfĕ-- ĭ- -ā-s ŭs ---ē -āz -ōō --ĭv -ōō f-ô-ə-ə.

13. She is a legal typist for a large law firm in the city.
    shē ĭz ə -ē-ə- -ĭpĭs- fô- ə -ä-j -ô fû-m ĭ- --ə sĭ-ĭ.

14. They will celebrate their twenty-fifth anniversary next month.
    --ā wĭ- se-əb-ā- --ĕ- -wĕ--ĭ fĭf-- ă-əvû-sərĭ -ĕ-s- mŭ---.

15. They live in a small apartment on the edge of town.
    --ā -ĭv ĭ- ə smô- əpä--mə-- ŏ-   ē ĕj ŭv -ou-.

88. Three-Word Drill

after, noon, afternoon

    I will meet you after work.
    Marie was born after John.

    Don't tell me it's noon already.
    The accident happened during my noon lunch hour.

    Let's leave early this afternoon.
    The baby still takes an afternoon nap.

ear, ring, earring

    Everything we tell her goes in one ear and out the other.
    Be careful what you say; children have big ears.

    Has anyone seen my key ring?
    That phone rings all day long.

    She lost an earring at the party.
    He gave her a pair of gold earrings for her birthday.

fare, well, farewell

    Bus fare will be increased five cents.
    Train fare is cheaper than plane fare.

    The coat was well worth the price.
    I'm not fortunate enough to own an oil well.

    It is to be his farewell performance.
    We were there to bid him farewell.

grand, stand, grandstand

    A grand time was had by all present.
    Give me the grand total of the weekly sales.

    We need another music stand.
    He has to stand trial next month.

    We have grandstand seats at the track.
    Some people paid fifty dollars for grandstand seats.

Rail, road, railroad

The entrance is by the split rail fence.
The meeting was held in the Brass Rail Bar.

The last two miles was over a dirt road.
It's a paved road all the way.

He worked for the railroad all his life.
The town is four miles from the railroad.

wall, paper, wallpaper

Let's install wall-to-wall carpeting.
It's a frame home with drywall construction.

Bring home an evening paper.
Bonded typewriter paper must be used.

We will wallpaper the bedrooms.
The entrance hall had dark green wallpaper.

89. Reading Sentences Beginning with *w* and *wh*

The sounds of *w* as in *will* and *way* and *wh* as in *who* occur only before a vowel. The lips are drawn together and puckered, protruding forward with the opening very narrow. When this movement appears at the beginning of a sentence, very often a question is being asked.

who

Who left this door open?
Who signed the letter?
Who will answer the phone?

what

What is the correct time?
What is the correct answer to the question?
What time will he be here?

why

Why did she leave without saying goodbye?
Why not make a duplicate copy for me?
Why don't we eat at the new restaurant tonight?

where

Where did I leave the keys to the car?
Where is the morning paper?
Where is their apartment located?

will

Will you bring home some postage stamps?
Will she drive to work today?
Will you meet me on the corner later?

when

When are you leaving on your vacation?
When does the fishing season open?
When does our lease expire?

was

Was that book worth reading?
Was he promoted to treasurer of the company?
Was his car badly damaged in the accident?

we

Will we vote for the bond issue?
We will wait for your answer.
We can shop after we have lunch.

which

Which one is the tallest?
Which house is yours?
Which pencil has the soft lead?

Quick Reference Guide

short *a* (*cat*)(*ă*)	Lips extend slightly at the corners; lip opening wide.
long *a* (*mate*) (*ā*) diphthong	Lip corners extend slightly with lip opening medium, followed quickly by a quick, narrow, natural opening.
broad *a* (*car*) (*ä*)	Lips natural; opening wide.
b (*baby*)	Lips natural.
soft *c* (*cent*)	Lip opening very narrow, hardly seen.
hard *c* (*call*)	Formed in throat; unseen lip movement.
d (*date*)	Seldom seen; tongue touches behind upper teeth.
short *e* (*let*)(*ĕ*)	Lips extend slightly at corners; lip opening medium.
long *e* (*be*)(*ē*)	Lips extend at corners; opening narrow.
f (*fence*)	Upper teeth touch lower lip.
hard *g* (*get*)	Formed in throat; unseen lip movement.
soft *g* (*gem*)	Lips pucker and thrust forward.
h (*hall*)	Unseen; breath expiration. Sometimes noticeable by falling of chest.
short *i* (*fit*)(*ĭ*)	Lip corners natural; lip opening narrow.
long *i* (*time*)(*i*) diphthong	Lips natural; lip opening wide followed by a quick, narrow opening.
j (*jade*)	Lips pucker and thrust forward.
k (*keen*)	Formed in throat; unseen lip movement.
l (*long*)	Seldom seen; tongue touches just behind upper teeth.
m (*moment*)	Lips natural.
n (*nine*)	Seldom seen; flat edge of tongue touches palate.
short *o* (*not*)(*ŏ*)	Lip corners natural; opening wide.
long *o* (*note*)(*ō*) diphthong	Double movement; opening wide. With a slight pucker, the lips narrow and become more puckered.
p (*paper*)	Lips natural.
q (*quick*)	*Q* is always followed by *u* and is pronounced *kw*. The *k* is unseen; for the *w* lips narrow and pucker.

r (*rare*)	Before vowel, lips pucker; after vowel, the *r* is slurred over.
s (*sent*)	Lip corners natural; very narrow opening, hardly seen with expiration of air.
t (*taste*)	Seldom seen; flat edge of tongue touches palate.
short *u* (*cup*)(*ŭ*)	Lip corners natural; lip opening medium (same movement as *oo* as in *blood*).
long *u* (*fuse*) (*ū*)	Lips pucker and thrust slightly forward with narrow opening.
v (*vest*)	Upper teeth touch lower lip.
w (*weed*); wh (*what*)	Lips pucker with a very narrow opening.
z (*zebra*)	Lip corners natural; lip opening narrow.
long *oo* (*moon*)(*ōō*)	Lips pucker; lip opening narrow.
short *oo* (*book*)(*ŏŏ*)	Lips pucker; lip opening medium.
ow (*now*) diphthong	Lips make a double movement; first a relaxed wide opening followed by a very puckered movement.
o (*ore*); *aw* (*raw*)	Lips pucker; lip opening wide.
oy (*toy*) diphthong	Lips make a double movement; first a slight pucker with a wide opening, followed quickly by a natural, narrow movement.
bl (*blank*); *br* (*brake*)	For the *b,* lips natural; for the *l,* tongue touches behind upper teeth; *r* is a roll of the tongue.
cl (*class*); *cr* (*cream*)	Hard *c* takes the *k* sound, lip opening very narrow; for the *l,* tongue touches behind upper teeth; *r* is a roll of the tongue.
dr (*drank*); *tr* (*trip*)	Lip opening narrow; for the *d* and *t,* tongue touches behind upper teeth; *r* is a roll of the tongue; both unseen movements.
fl (*floor*); *fr* (*frame*)	For the *f,* upper teeth touch lower lip; for the *l,* tongue touches behind upper teeth; the *r* is a roll of the tongue; *l* and *r* are unseen.
gr (*green*)	Hard *g* is a throat sound; *r* is a roll of the tongue; both unseen.
ng (*song*); *nk* (*mink*)	Formed in throat; lip movement unseen.

pl (*place*); *pr* (*price*)	For the *p*, lips natural; for the *l*, tongue touches behind upper teeth; the *r* is a roll of the tongue.
sl (slate)	For the *s*, lip corners natural; opening very narrow; for the *l*, tongue touches behind upper teeth; both unseen.
sm (*small*); *sp* (*spell*)	(Homophonous) for the *s*, lip corners natural; opening very narrow; for the *m* and *p*, lips natural.
sn (*snake*); *st* (*stack*); *sw* (*sweep*)	For the *s*, lip opening narrow; for the *n* and *t*, tongue touches upper teeth; for the *w*, lips pucker and extend forward slightly.
shr (*shred*)	For the *sh*, lips pucker and thrust forward with a small opening; the *r* is a roll of the tongue.
spl (*splash*); *spr* (*spring*)	For the *s*, lip corners natural with a very narrow opening; for the *p*, lips natural; for the *l*, tongue touches behind upper teeth; the *r*, is a quick, slurring roll of tongue.
str (*string*)	For the *s*, lip corners natural with a very narrow opening; for the *t*, tongue touches back of upper teeth; the *r* is an unseen, slurred roll of the tongue.
th (*thaw*)	Tongue touches upper teeth; lip movement unseen.
thr (*thread*)	For the *th*, lip corners natural, narrow opening, tongue touching upper teeth; the *r* is a slurred overroll of the tongue.